KU-496-248

CONTENTS

❖

ABOUT LONDON TRANSPORT

THE UNDERGROUND

With trains running every few minutes on most lines, the Underground provides a frequent and reliable service, 20 hours a day. Once you are armed with a copy of the Tube Map (on the inside front cover of this book and also available free from ticket offices and Travel Information Centres), finding your way around the Tube is straightforward.

Tickets have to be purchased before you travel on the Tube, otherwise you are liable to a penalty fare of £10. Tickets can be purchased through ticket machines in the stations or from the station's booking office. Fares are based on a zonal system; further details are available from all ticket offices.

Most central London stations now have automatic exit and entry ticket gates. Put your ticket into the automatic gate, then take it out at the top, at which point the gate will open and you can walk through. If you have completed your journey the machine will keep the ticket, but valid Travelcards will be returned by the machine on the automatic gate.

THE BUSES

London's famous buses now come in all shapes and sizes. Many are still red but other companies run buses in their own colours for London Transport. The London Transport Service symbol on the front of those buses that are not red tells you that Travelcards are accepted.

There are two types of bus stop: Compulsory (white background) and Request (red background). Buses will stop automatically to pick up at Compulsory stops unless the bus is full. Buses will only stop at Request stops if you signal to the bus driver by putting your arm out, or if you ring the bell while on the bus.

NIGHT BUSES

If you stay out late you can always get home by using one of the special night buses. These are identified by letter N before the number. Many of the night buses follow daytime routes, but others have their own routes. All night buses (except N31) pass through Trafalgar Square to the popular entertainment areas. But remember that One-Day Travelcards and Weekend Travelcards are not accepted on night buses and fares are higher than during the day. All bus stops become Request stops at night.

In association with London Transport

KIDS' LONDON

FRANCESCA COLLIN

WARD LOCK

AUTHOR'S ACKNOWLEDGEMENTS

Thank you to the staff at the many museums, galleries, tourist attractions,
theatres, cinemas, shops, restaurants and local councils who all helped with my
research. I would also like to acknowledge the support of Charlotte Howard,
Emily van Eesteren and Jane Birch, as well as that of my family,
particularly Simon and Natasha Collin.

A WARD LOCK BOOK
First published in the UK 1997 by Ward Lock
Wellington House, 125 Strand
LONDON WC2R 0BB

A Cassell Imprint
Copyright © Volume Ward Lock 1997
© Text Francesca Collin 1997
© Posters and advertisements London Transport Museum 1997

Distributed in the United States
by Sterling Publishing Co., Inc.
387 Park Avenue South, New York, NY 10016–8810

A British Library Cataloguing in Publication Data block for this
book may be obtained from the British Library
ISBN 0 7063 7514 9

Managing Editor Jane Birch
Designed by Richard Carr
Printed and bound in Spain

❖

TRAVELCARDS AND SEASON TICKETS

You can purchase Travelcards valid for one or seven days, but One-Day Travelcards can be subject to early morning rush hour restrictions. Travelcards are accepted on all London Transport buses, Underground lines, Docklands Light Railway and most trains, within the zones you have paid for. Period Travelcards, which do not have rush hour restrictions, are valid for one week, one month or any period up to a year.

The Family Travelcard is a One-Day ticket for the family with all the benefits of the One-Day Travelcard, but which saves you even more money. You can use the Tube, buses (not night buses) displaying the London Transport buses sign, Docklands Light Railway and any rail service within the travel zones selected.

The weekend Travelcard is valid for the two days of the weekend or two consecutive days during a weekend with a public holiday. It has the same validity as the Family Travelcard.

The Carnet is a book of ten tickets for Zone 1 only. It saves money if you are travelling solely within Zone 1, and is available for adults and children.

TRAVEL INFORMATION

London Transport Travel Information Centres (TICs) offer a wide range of services, including maps, phone cards, souvenirs and sightseeing tours. They can be found at:

RAIL STATIONS

Euston, Victoria

BUS STATIONS

Hammersmith, West Croydon

HEATHROW AIRPORT TERMINALS

Terminal 1, 2 and 4 Arrivals

UNDERGROUND STATIONS

Heathrow 1, 2, 3, King's Cross, Liverpool Street, Oxford Circus, Piccadilly Circus, St James's Park

LT TRAVEL INFORMATION CALL CENTRE

You can telephone 0171 222 1234, 24 hours a day (except Christmas Day) for up-to-the-minute information on all aspects of public transport within the Greater London area.

RAIL

Those travelling from outside London can reach the city by rail and many of the services connect with the Underground network. While you are more dependent on timetables with rail, there are fewer stops so distances are covered more quickly. The main stations in London are: Charing Cross, Euston, King's Cross, Liverpool Street, Paddington, St Pancras, Victoria and Waterloo, which now gives you access to Europe through the Channel Tunnel.

INTRODUCTION

CHILDREN who live outside London have much to envy their city cousins. Over six million people live in the capital and the city offers an almost unrivalled range of activities and entertainments specifically aimed at children.

Perhaps the best starting point for a child is to visit some of the most famous London landmarks, such as Big Ben, Buckingham Palace or the Tower of London. These and many more places are all described in *Kids' London*, along with hundreds of ideas for things to do. Getting about is an important consideration – a London Transport Family Travelcard will give you the freedom to roam while a boat trip adds an element of adventure.

Museums and galleries are roaring into the twenty-first century with ever more exciting exhibitions and interactive displays. Many also organize excellent weekend, half-term and holiday workshops and activities for kids – a great way to pass a wet (or even a sunny) afternoon.

London isn't all buildings and landmarks though – there is plenty to see and do outdoors too. There are some wonderful parks scattered all across London, and many have excellent playgrounds to enjoy. For the more adventurous, explore one of the established 'country' walks set up around London's perimeter, which

Piccadilly Circus

will give you the chance to see some beautiful plants, birds and possibly the occasional wild animal. For a guaranteed chance of seeing some interesting animals, visit the London Zoo or a city farm.

Kids are also spoilt for choice with indoor entertainment. As well as showing the latest blockbuster movies, many London cinemas have Kids' Clubs on Saturdays where they screen old and new children's classic films. There is some great drama staged for children too, especially at such theatres as the Polka Theatre in Wimbledon and the Unicorn Arts in the West End.

Food is an important priority for most children, and the range of munchies available at London's eateries should be broad enough to tempt even the fussiest palate. There are numerous tempting shops catering especially for children too.

But, in spite of all the glitzy attractions of London, having fun doesn't need to break the bank. Many of the places to go and things to do suggested in *Kids' London* are free or cost very little, and I have selected some of the best in the section 'Days out for free (almost)' on pages 168–171. Here, you will also find some other 'recipe' ideas for great family days out in town – I hope that these and the rest of this book prove a useful guide to kids' London!

Francesca Collin

Note

As some activities are arranged at short notice and opening days and times are also subject to change, it is advisable to check details in advance.

Symbols Used in This Book

⊖	Underground station	P	Parking available
🚉	Railway station	♿	Wheelchair access
DLR	Docklands Light Railway station	£	Small charge – less than £6
🚌	Buses (where several buses serve a particular place, only the major ones are given)	££	Moderate charge – £6 and above
〰	Boat	✺	Cycling permitted

❖

WHERE TO GO FIRST

CHAPTER ONE

LONDON LANDMARKS

A S several of London's most famous landmarks are centuries old, the following brief outline of how the city has developed over the years may help to stimulate children's interest in the capital. London's history began almost 2,000 years ago, when a walled city called Londinium was founded here by the Romans in about AD 43. When they left Britain in AD 61, the city was abandoned. The Anglo-Saxons built a new city, called Lundunwick, outside the Roman city walls in the area that is now the Strand. The city grew in importance as a major port

and over several hundred years was regularly invaded by the Danes from the north. Eventually, the city moved back behind the safety of the old Roman walls, which were repaired and refortified. By 1066, the city was thriving once again and a royal palace and abbey had been built at Westminster.

During the Middle Ages, London continued to develop in importance as a centre for international trade and commerce. By the early seventeenth century about 225,000 people lived here. However, the numerous ships that docked at London did not just bring spices and exotic goods from abroad, they brought rats and those rats carried the bubonic plague, which struck London in 1665. Within a year it had killed about 100,000 people, almost a third of London's population. By 1666 the disease was controlled, but then fresh disaster struck. On 2 September a fire broke out at a bakery in Pudding Lane. By nightfall of the same day, 300 houses nearby and half of those on London Bridge were in flames. The fire continued to rage for five days, by which time it had destroyed three-quarters of the city.

Over the next hundred years the elegant squares and terraces of Georgian London were built over the charred remains of the medieval city. In the nineteenth century the Victorians continued to develop London, building the Houses of Parliament and museums such as the Victoria & Albert Museum, as well as houses and tenements in every part of the capital for the growing population.

In the Second World War London was heavily bombed and the subsequent rebuilding changed the character of many parts of the metropolis. The city has seen other significant changes in the twentieth century too. The Docklands, which for hundreds of years had been bustling centres of international trade, went into decline from the 1960s when goods began arriving in containers. Ships no longer needed to come all the way up the River Thames to dock, but could unload at coastal ports, the containers being put straight on to lorries and taken to their destinations. Fortunately, the Docklands have adapted to changing needs, an extensive programme of rebuilding and regeneration making them important business and financial centres, as well as popular residential areas.

ROYAL LONDON

Of the dozens of traditional ceremonies that take place all over London each year, royal ceremonial events are among the most spectacular. It is astonishing to think that many have been carried out in the same way for centuries. Events such as the Changing of the Guard were originally a means for the monarchs to demonstrate their military power as a warning to potential enemies. See page 158.

Buckingham Palace
St James's Park, SW1 (0171 839 1377)
In 1762 George III bought Buckingham House from the Duke of Buckingham. His son, George IV, had the building substantially redesigned by Nash and the work was completed during the reign of Queen Victoria. The palace is still used as the official London residence of the Royal Family, as well as the centre of operations for their staff.

Buckingham Palace

Since 1993, the palace has thrown open its doors every August and September to allow people into its State Rooms – the Grand Hall, Throne Room, Green Drawing Room, State Dining Room, Music Room and the Silk Tapestry Room – along with several galleries. It is a fascinating chance to see many items from the Royal Collection and the rooms where important Heads of State are entertained.

Just around the corner from Buckingham Palace are the royal mews. These house the Queen's horses and the elegant carriages used on state occasions.

⊖/🚇 Victoria

🚌 1, 16, 24, 52, 73

♿ (Palace and Mews)

Open: Palace: August–September, daily, 9.30 a.m.–5.30 p.m. (last admission 4.15 p.m.); ticket office opens at 9.00 a.m.

££ (under-fives free)

Mews: late March–late September, Tuesday–Thursday, 12 noon–4.00 p.m.; early October–late March, Wednesday 12 noon–4.00 p.m.

£

Hampton Court Palace

East Molesey, Surrey (0181 781 9500)

Hampton Court Palace was given to Henry VIII by Cardinal Wolsey. Later monarchs added to the beautiful buildings. With great gardens to explore too and the river close by, it makes an excellent day out.

Hampton Court has been divided into six different routes, which make it far easier to enjoy and appreciate. Don't be surprised if you bump into some unusual-looking characters – the guides here dress up in Tudor costume, which helps to give an atmosphere of life in the palace and adds some colour to a visit. It is well worth joining the guided tours around each part as the guides are full of fascinating information about the palace. Tours usually start in the Clock Court and take place every couple of hours (check the timetable when you arrive).

In Henry VIII's State Apartments you will see the grand rooms for dining and waiting upon the king. Most visitors to the palace in Tudor times would never have gone past the Great Hall as only a few of the king's most trusted men would be allowed close contact with him.

The Queen's State Apartments were intended for Mary II, who sadly died before the palace was completed. They were decorated and furnished in later reigns.

The smaller Georgian Rooms provide an insight into the lives and pastimes of the Georgian court.

Following the fire in 1986, the rooms in the King's Apartment's, built and decorated for William III, have now been restored to their original appearance, containing mementoes of both his public and private life.

The Wolsey Rooms and the Renaissance Picture Gallery, built for Cardinal Wolsey, now display important Renaissance paintings from Her Majesty the Queen's collection.

The reconstruction of the huge Tudor kitchens is unrivalled anywhere in the country. It is so realistic you can really imagine what they would have been like on a busy feast day in Henry VIII's time. To appreciate the scale of the kitchens, examine the detailed model first, which explains the function of each room. Inside the kitchen complex, you will see the huge cooking areas with massive fires where the meat was cooked, turned on the spit by young boys. The fires are lit every day – but fortunately spit boys are no longer employed to turn the spits! The kitchens also include a herb room, a butcher's and a pâtisserie area where the king's favourite cakes were made.

The palace gardens are well worth visiting too (see page 126). Facilities include a shop and cafés.

🚇 Hampton Court, Hampton Wick

🚌 R68, 111, 216, 726

〰 From Westminster, Charing Cross, Richmond, Kingston

Limited ♿

Open: mid-October–March, daily, 9.30a.m. – 4.30 p.m. (Monday, from 10.15 a.m.); April–mid-October, daily, 9.30 a.m.–6.00 p.m. (Monday, from 10.15 a.m.); last admission 45 minutes before closing time; closed 24–26 December

£–££

HM Tower of London

Tower Hill, EC3 (0171 709 0765)

The Tower of London is one of the city's oldest landmarks. Built by William I as a fortress, it has also served as the Royal Mint, Royal Observatory and Armoury and as a prison. The Royal Armouries are now divided between three sites: the Tower of London, Portsmouth (artillery) and Leeds (arms and armour).

The Tower of London is currently reorganizing its collections in the White Tower, which was built as a fortress and a palace to embody royal power and splendour. It continued in that role as an armoury and arsenal, and later as a public showplace. The first of the permanent exhibitions which tell the tower's story will be opened to the public towards the end of 1997 and the rest by early 1998.

In the meantime two temporary exhibitions have been created for visitors, featuring a selection of items from the forthcoming permanent display. One shows the lavish royal splendour of six armours produced for Henry VIII and the Stuart kings and princes alongside the harsher face of royal power represented by instruments of torture and punishment such as the block used for the last public beheading in England, in 1747. Perhaps more suitable for children is the second exhibition, the 'Images of the Tower' in the New Armouries building. On display are the weapons of Henry VIII's bodyguard and a number of armours which belonged to members of the king's court. Of particular interest to children is a model jousting horse which can be mounted to give you a head-on view of the famous armour for man and horse made for Henry VIII in 1514. You can also measure yourself against an armour made for a giant of 2.05 metres (6 feet 9 inches) and another thought to have been made for a dwarf in 1610.

❖

In the medieval Palace above Traitor's Gate the rooms have been carefully restored to reveal what life was like in the Tower in the 1280s during the reign of Edward I. Guides dressed in replica medieval costume are present in every room to explain the contents and to demonstrate thirteenth-century activities such as calligraphy and quill-making.

The crowning glories of the building are the Crown Jewels – the 106.5 carat Koh-i-noor dates back to the thirteenth century and is set in the crown of Queen Elizabeth, the Queen Mother. However, the 'jewel in the crown' is the jewel in the Sceptre with Cross, symbolizing the monarch's power. It is topped by the First Star of Africa, the world's largest cut diamond at 530 carats.

Guided tours of the Tower (which take place at regular intervals during the day) include a visit to Traitor's Gate and St Thomas's Tower, the Middle Tower, Byward Tower, Bloody Tower (where, according to legend, the Little Princes were murdered in 1485) and the Bell Tower. Tower Green was the site of many executions and the burial place for the bodies. Before they were buried, the heads were placed on pikes and displayed at the southern gateway to London Bridge.

DLR Tower Gateway, Tower Hill

⊖ Tower Hill

▣ Fenchurch Street

🚌 15, 42, 78, 100

Limited ♿

Open: March–October, Monday–Saturday, 9.00 a.m–6.00 p.m.; Sunday, 10.00 a.m–6.00 p.m; November–February, Monday–Saturday, 9.00 a.m.–5.00 p.m; Sunday, 10.00 a.m.–5.00p.m.

££

Kensington Palace

The State Apartments, Kensington Gardens, W8 (0171 937 9561)
In 1689 William III moved to what was then a wealthy merchant's house, Nottingham House, and established Kensington Palace in the heart of royal hunting grounds. George II was the last reigning monarch to reside in the palace but today various members of the royal family still live there. Their apartments are closed to the public, but it is possible to visit several State Apartments and to see the Royal Ceremonial Dress Collection. Dating from the mid-eighteenth century onwards, this is a collection of uniforms, court dresses and wedding dresses worn by the royal family and their court. There is a shop.

⊖ High Street Kensington, Notting Hill Gate, Queensway

🚌 9, 10, 12, 52, 94

Limited ♿

Open: May–September, daily, tours only, 9.45 a.m.–3.30 p.m. (last tour)

£

Westminster Abbey

Dean's Yard, SW1 (0171 222 5152)

While St Paul's Cathedral is very much a church for the people of London, Westminster Abbey is particularly associated with the kings and queens of England.

The first church to be built on this site was constructed about AD 605 for a Saxon king. Edward the Confessor, however, is usually regarded as the founder of the church. He was crowned here and so has every monarch been since. Elizabeth II was crowned here in June 1953 and the service lasted a staggering four hours. Until the time of George III the Abbey was also where English monarchs were buried. The Abbey contains monuments to many of Britain's leading artists, writers and statesmen, and people such as William Shakespeare, the scientist Sir Isaac Newton, and the explorer David Livingstone.

Once you have wandered through the interior of the Abbey, make for the cloisters (situated off the south aisle of the nave). Here there is a brass rubbing centre (see page 48); also a good coffee bar for refreshments.

Next to the Abbey is Westminster School, a boys' public school, which is closely linked with the Abbey and was founded in 1560 by Elizabeth I. Boys from the school form part of the Abbey's choir.

Also worth visiting while you are here is the museum, which has effigies of such monarchs as Charles II, Elizabeth I and William III, as well as various important dignitaries. Modelled from death masks, they give a realistic image of what these people really looked like. The museum also houses a collection of Romanesque carvings, a set of replica Coronation regalia and drawings by Sir Christopher Wren.

Bookings for the guided Super Tours can be made in advance by phoning 0171 222 7100. These include admission to the Chapter House, Treasury and Museum, and leave the enquiry desk in the nave at specified times from Monday to Saturday subject to demand.

Westminster Abbey is usually particularly busy with visitors in the morning (9.00 a.m.–10.30 a.m.), as many people visit it before moving on to Buckingham Palace to watch the Changing of the Guard at 11.00 a.m. Therefore it is sensible to plan your visit for later in the day.

⊖ Westminster

🚌 3, 11, 12, 24, 77A, 211

♿

Open: Abbey: Monday–Friday, 9.00 a.m.–4.45 p.m. (Wednesday, also 6.00 p.m–7.45 p.m., the only time amateur photography is allowed); Saturday, 9.00 a.m.–2.45 p.m. and 3.45 pm–5.45 p.m; Sunday, open only for worship; last admission 45 minutes before closing times

££ (cheaper on Wednesday after 6.00 p.m)

❖

The Ceremony of the Keys

Each evening the gates of the Tower of London are locked by the Chief Warder of the Yeoman Warders, who is ceremonially challenged by a sentry as he nears the Bloody Tower. At 10.00 p.m. the Last Post is sounded and the Chief Warder hands over his keys to the Resident Governor and Major in the Queen's House.

It is only possible to watch this ceremony by making written application to the Clerk of Ceremony of the Keys, Queen's House, HM Tower of London, EC3N 4AB.

POLITICS AND GOVERNMENT

Running from Trafalgar Square to Parliament Square, Whitehall houses the government buildings where the administration of the country is carried out. Halfway down Whitehall is Downing Street with the official residences of the Prime Minister and the Chancellor of the Exchequer. The public are not now allowed into Downing Street for security reasons, but it is worth pausing at the entrance to the street – you might catch a glimpse of the Prime Minister being driven to the House of Commons for a debate or Prime Minister's Question Time.

Houses of Parliament

Parliament Square, SW1 (0171 219 3000)
Officially known as the Palace of West-minster, it was rebuilt from 1834 onwards, after a fire destroyed most of the original buildings. The only parts to have survived are the Great Hall, built by William II between 1097 and 1099, and the crypt and cloisters of St Stephen's Chapel.

The palace was a royal residence from the reign of Edward the Confessor to the reign of Henry VII and it is now the seat of govern-ment. The buildings are immense, covering 3.2 hectares (8 acres), with eleven courtyards, 3 kilometres (2 miles) of corridors and over 1,000 rooms. Big Ben, the most famous clock tower in Britain, was probably named after Sir Benjamin Hill, who commissioned the enormous bell and completed work on the 96-metre (316-foot) tower in 1859.

Although the building is not open to the public, you can arrange to go on a tour. British citizens must write to their MP, while citizens from other countries have to apply by writing to the Public Information Office of the House of Commons.

It is also possible to watch your MP at work in a Parliamentary debate. The galleries are open to the public and priority is given to those with tickets (obtainable from your MP or, for overseas citizens, from your embassy or High Commission).

Every autumn, at the end of the summer recess, the Queen officially opens Parliament and makes a speech outlining the programme of proposed legislation for the next year. The public are not admitted but can watch the arrival and departure of the royal party in the state coaches.

⊖ Westminster

🚌 3, 11, 24, 77A

♿

Open: by arrangement only (see above)

Free (charge if you hire a guide)

THE CITY

Popularly known as the 'Square Mile', the City was the heart of medieval London, whereas it is now primarily a financial centre of international importance. Over the centuries many cities have had craft companies or guilds. However, the Livery Companies of the City of London are unique in their number and diversity and in maintaining their close links with the government of the City. Guilds were first formed in London in medieval times as a means of supervising quality control, protecting customers, employers and employees by searching out inferior work and goods of bad quality and punishing offenders. By preventing unlimited competition a standard of wages and conditions was preserved.

Guild members came to be known as liverymen because they wore a distinctive livery or uniform. Livery companies have traditionally played an important part in the organization of the City and they alone can select the Lord Mayor and the Sheriffs. Today, many livery companies also have an active role in raising money for charities and educational activities.

There are currently ninety-seven livery companies in the City, including the Baker's Company, which was first formed as a guild in 1155, the Goldsmiths' Company, which was first mentioned in 1180, and more recently formed companies such as the Air Pilots and Air Navigators' Guild, which began in 1929. Entry to any livery company is possible by only three methods, which helps retain its exclusivity and perhaps its air of mystery: first, by being the son of a liveryman, the second is by apprenticeship, which means serving for a period of time in a particular trade, and the third is known as redemption, which means paying to join.

The only way for the public to visit the halls of the livery companies is to apply to the City Information Office (0171 606 3030) early in the year for part of the small allocation of tickets which it receives each February. The companies participating in the scheme include the Goldsmiths, the Tallow Chandlers, the Skinners, the Fishmongers and the Haberdashers.

It is also possible to visit the impressive Fishmongers' Hall at the north end of London Bridge at other times by contacting their archivist on 0171 626 3531.
Free (donations welcome)

Bank of England

Threadneedle Street, EC2 (0171 601 4878)
The Bank of England is the central bank of the United Kingdom and serves as both bank to the government and to its banking system. Founded in 1694, the Bank of England started as a commercial bank with private shareholders and developed a large private banking business. It was not until 1946 that it was brought into state ownership.

It is not open to the public, but the Bank of England Museum is well worth visiting (see page 62).
◿ Bank
🚍 8, 11, 22B, 133

The Monument

Monument Street, EC3 (0171 626 2717)
Built to commemorate the Great Fire of 1666, the Monument is situated close to the northern approach to London Bridge and stands in a small open space now known as Monument Yard on the east side of Fish Street Hill. This was once the site of St Margaret's Church, which had been the first to perish in the Great Fire, so that its height of 62 metres (202 feet) could be equal to its distance from the baker's house in Pudding Lane where the fire began.
◿ Monument
🚉 London Bridge
🚍 15, 22A, 35, 40, 48
No ♿
Open: April–September, Monday–Friday, 9.00 a.m–5.40 p.m. Saturday and Sunday, 2.00 p.m.–5.40 p.m.; October–March, Monday–Saturday, 9.00 a.m.–3.40 p.m.
£

The Monument

St Paul's Cathedral

St Paul's Churchyard, EC4 (0171 236 4128)

It is remarkable to think that St Paul's Cathedral was the work of just one architect, Sir Christopher Wren, between 1675 and 1710. Although a church has stood on the site since AD 604, the present cathedral was built after the earlier building had been destroyed in the Great Fire of 1666.

As with many renowned churches and cathedrals, St Paul's contains numerous monuments in its crypt. The grave of Admiral Nelson, who led the British navy to a famous victory at Trafalgar in 1805, is among the most interesting. His coffin was made from the main mast of the French flagship defeated at the Battle of Aboukir. There are also monuments to English painters such as Reynolds and Constable.

Perhaps the most striking feature of this amazing building is the dome, which is 111.25 metres (365 feet) high to the tip of the lantern and 30.48 metres (100 feet) in diameter inside – the second largest in the world. If you climb up the dome, you will first come to the Whispering Gallery. It is so called because a faint whisper against the wall on one side can be heard on the other side.

Climbing further up you will reach the Stone Gallery, which runs outside the dome. From here on a clear day you will have a magnificent view across London – it is worth using the telescope for an even better view. If you have the energy and a good head for heights, continue up to the narrow Golden Gallery at the top of the dome, by which time you will have climbed 530 steps.

ϴ St Paul's

🚌 8, 11, 15, 25, 26

Limited ♿

Open: Monday–Saturday, 8.30 a.m.–4.30 p.m. (last admission 4.00 pm.), subject to closures due to services; Sunday, services; guided tours at 11.00 a.m., 11.30 a.m., and 2.00 p.m, lasting 1½–2 hours (additional charge or combined tickets)

£–££

The dome of St Paul's Cathedral

Street Names

Cheapside was at one time an open market and the surrounding streets still bear the names of the items once displayed for sale in them. On the north side are Milk Street, Wood Street, Ironmonger Lane and Honey Lane, and to the south is Bread Street. Poultry is a continuation of Cheapside. The name Cheapside is derived from the Anglo-Saxon 'ceapian', meaning to sell or bargain. Shoe Lane, however, has nothing to do with shoemakers, but was named after an ancient well, 'Sho well', which was sited on the north end of the street.

Houndsditch, on the eastern side of the City towards Aldgate, is named after the old ditch that surrounded the city wall. Crutched Friars is a crooked street which derived its name from a former monastery of the Friars of the Holy Cross. A monastery was established here in medieval times when the royal court resided at the Tower of London. Threadneedle Street, which runs past the Stock Exchange, probably takes its name either from the three needles that appear in the arms of the Needlemakers' Livery Company or from the thread and needle used by the Merchant Taylors Livery Company. In Roman times Cornhill was the site of a basilica. Later, in medieval times, it became a grain market.

OTHER SIGHTS

British Telecom Tower

Cleveland Street, W1

When it was built in 1964 this was the tallest building in London at 188.67 metres (619 feet). It was built this height to allow it to broadcast television and radio signals clearly above all the surrounding buildings. Today, it is no longer London's tallest building; that honour has gone to the Nat West Tower in the City. Sadly, the public are not allowed inside either landmark.

ϴ Great Portland Street

🚌 C2, 18, 27, 30, 135

Covent Garden

WC2

Covent Garden is one of London's most lively areas. Bustling with shoppers, street entertainers and tourists, there is always plenty to see, do and buy.

The old covered market halls form the centerpiece of the area. From 1656 to 1974 Covent Garden was London's best-known fruit and vegetable market, where farmers would come up from the country early every morning to sell their produce to shopkeepers and restaurants. Since the 1970s this market has been based in Vauxhall and Covent Garden has been transformed. Today the covered area has been converted into dozens of great shops and cafés. You will also find craft stalls, selling all sorts of items from brightly coloured hand-knitted jumpers to pottery and jewellery, displayed on original trading stands. There are more craft and clothes stalls around the outside of the market buildings too, as well as a separate covered market, known as the Jubilee Market. Shops of interest to children in the area include the Doc Marten shoe store in the Piazza and Stanfords map shop in Long Acre.

Covent Garden is right at the heart of London's Theatreland, with the Theatre Royal Drury Lane and the Royal Opera House just around the corner and other theatres a few minutes walk away. Traditionally, it has been well known for street entertainers too, and the first Punch and Judy show was performed here in 1662. Today, there is an annual Punch and Judy Festival held every May to commemorate this (see page 161).

Jugglers, mime artists, clowns and musicians perform every day in the area near St Paul's church which looks over the Piazza (the outdoor area around the market) and in the covered part of the market. It is great fun to sit and watch them while licking an ice-cream and, of course, it needn't cost you anything. However, remember that this is how they make a living, so feel free to donate generously if you think they are worth it!

Good places for families to eat around Covent Garden include Cranks vegetarian restaurant (open daily, 9.00 a.m.–8.30 p.m.) and the Market Café, which offers a variety of fast food and a self-service area in the heart of the market halls (open daily, 10.00 a.m.–12 midnight).

"Now that Covent Garden Station is open on Sundays, most of my audience have come by Tube"

COVENT GARDEN

As well as the shops and cafés there are plenty of other attractions in this area, such as the London Transport Museum in the old flower market (see page 66), the Theatre Museum in Tavistock Street, see page 61) and the Cabaret Mechanical Theatre in the covered market.

When you have explored this part of Covent Garden, cross over Long Acre (the road that runs alongside Covent Garden tube) and over into Neal Street and Neal's Yard. This is a pedestrianized area with plenty of interesting shops to potter around. Among the best are The Kite Store (see page 87), the Bead Shop (see page 183) and Bladerubber Stamps, which sells every kind of rubber stamp from flowers to cartoon characters (2 Neal's Yard, WC2, 0171 379 7391, open Monday–Saturday, 10.30 a.m.–6.00 p.m., Monday from 11.00 a.m.).

⊖ Covent Garden, Leicester Square

🚌 6, 9, 11, 13, 15, 23, 26

Cabaret Mechanical Theatre

At 33 The Market (0171 379 7691) you will find an unusual display of mechanical models, known as automata, all designed by contemporary craftsmen. Among the more bizarre interactive models is 'Krankenstein', a scary Frankenstein model. You have to crank a handle to get the model going and it will then make blood-curdling noises. Also, to test your nerve, there is a model snake in a cage which appears to 'bite' you if it catches your hand in its cage!
No ♿

Open: school holidays, daily 10.00 a.m.–7.00 p.m.; all other times, Monday – Saturday 10.00 a.m.–6.00 p.m.; Sunday, 11.00 a.m.–7.00 p.m.

Harrods

Knightsbridge, SW3 (0171 730 1234)

Harrods is probably the most famous store in London. It started life in the mid-nineteenth century as a grocery shop and by the end of the century was already a major department store. Today, it claims to sell almost everything 'within reason' and is particularly well known for its luxury products. Some of the best parts to go and look at are the magnificent Food Hall and the extensive toy department, where you will find every type of toy under the sun, from a giant-size cuddly teddy bear to the latest computer game.

⊖ Knightsbridge

🚌 C1, 9, 14, 52, 74

♿

Open: Saturday, Monday and Tuesday, 10.00 a.m.–6.00 p.m.; Wednesday–Friday, 10.00 a.m.–7.00 p.m.

Heathrow Airport

Uxbridge, Middlesex (0181 759 4321)

Aircraft enthusiasts have an opportunity of seeing Concorde arriving or departing at Heathrow Airport. There are plenty of other flights during the day to watch from the spectators' viewing area. For more information on what's going on at the airport, go to the visitor centre, where there is an interactive exhibition covering Heathrow's past, present and future. You can see behind the scenes and experience life in the cockpit, in cargo and customs, and even make brass rubbings of aircraft profiles.

A more unexpected attraction of Heathrow Airport is the Causeway Nature Reserve. Developed from a former gravel pit, the reserve comprises a lake, scrubland and woodland. It is a good example of a mutually beneficial relationship between industry and the environment as the lake is one of three 'balancing ponds' which filter and clean surface run-off water from the runways at Heathrow Airport. Once the water is cleaned, it gradually enters the River Crane.

Θ Heathrow Terminals 1, 2, 3 or 4

🚌 43, 105, 111, 140, 285

P short-term car park

♿

Open: Airport, daily, 24 hours; viewing area, July–September, daily, 9.00 a.m.–7.00 p.m., October–June, daily, 9.00 a.m.–dusk

Piccadilly Circus

W1

At the heart of London's West End, Piccadilly Circus is overlooked by buildings covered with the famous flashing illuminated signs, advertising everything from Coca Cola to Kodak camera film. The centre point is a fountain and the statue of Eros (the Angel of Christian Charity), which is surrounded by steps and a pedestrian area, usually swarming with young tourists (see also the Trocadero, page 35).

Θ Piccadilly Circus

🚌 3, 12, 14, 19, 38

♿

Trafalgar Square
WC2

The high point (literally) of Trafalgar Square is Nelson's Column, built to commemorate Admiral Nelson, who was killed during his victorious battle against Napoleon's French navy off Trafalgar in Spain in 1805. On top of the 56-metre (185-foot) high column is a statue of Nelson with one arm and one eye – he lost them both in battle. At the foot of the column are brass reliefs showing battle scenes cast from the defeated French cannons at the Battle of Trafalgar. At its base lie four lions. Modelled by the artist Sir Edwin Landseer, they were cast from the cannons of battleships. On 21 October each year there is a service under the column to commemorate Nelson.

At Christmas time Norway always sends a huge Christmas tree that stands in Trafalgar Square, in gratitude for Britain's help during the Second World War (see page 167).

Ｏ Charing Cross, Embankment
Ｅ Charing Cross
Ｂ 9, 11, 23, 24, 29
ﾋ

Colourful Figures

The Yeoman Warders, or 'Beefeaters', who guard the Tower of London, still wear Tudor costume, with blue tunics carrying the sovereign's monogram on the chest. The origin of the name 'Beefeater' is not clear. One possible reason is that the Yeoman Warders wear the same uniform as the yeomen who once served the buffet at St James's Palace and became known as 'Buffetiers'.

The Chelsea Pensioners, veteran soldiers who live at the Royal Hospital in Chelsea, are regularly seen around the King's Road. They wear the traditional red uniform in summer, along with their highly polished medals.

Pearly Kings and Queens – a nickname dating back to Victorian times – were the elected leaders of the costermongers, who sold fruit and vegetables in the street. They traditionally dressed up in elaborate costumes studded with innumerable pearl buttons. The title can be passed down through families and today Pearly Kings and Queens devote their time to charitable activities.

LONDON'S WATERWAYS

THE THAMES

The Thames is one of the most famous landmarks in London. Historically, it was an important trade route, allowing ships to come right into the heart of the city to unload. As a result, London developed around the Thames, initially north of the river and then, as more bridges were built, it spread south.

Before modern means of transport were developed, Londoners regularly used to travel on boats up and down the river. Today, the river is used mainly for pleasure and a river cruise is a relaxing and pleasurable way to see some of the best sights in London.

Downstream (towards the mouth of the Thames) is the oldest part of London, including Westminster, the City, the Tower of London and Greenwich, along with the regenerated Docklands. Upstream, a trip will take you past Chelsea and Battersea, Hammersmith and Chiswick to the almost rural areas of Richmond, Teddington and finally Hampton. At Teddington you will pass through a lock and from here onwards the river is non-tidal.

The Tower Bridge Experience
SE1 (0171 378 1928)
There are splendid views from the enclosed high-level walkway across the top of the towers – you can either walk up the 200 steps or take the lift. There is also a museum with various interesting exhibits, plus Victorian engine rooms with the

original steam engines that used to open the bridge to let ships through. Today, the hydraulic lifting mechanisms are powered by electricity.

⊖ Tower Hill

DLR Tower Gateway

🚌 15, 42, 78, 100

♿

Open: April–October, daily, 10.00 a.m.–6.30 p.m. (last admission 5.15 p.m.); November–March, daily, 9.30 a.m.–6.00 p.m. (last admission 4.45 p.m.)

£–££

Thames Barrier Visitors' Centre

Unity Way, Woolwich, SE18 (0181 854 1373)

Flooding was a major problem for London for centuries; in 1928 fourteen people drowned in central London and in 1953 there was a disastrous flood along the east coast and Thames estuary, with the loss of 300 lives. If the flood had reached central London, the result could have been even more of a catastrophe.

A way to prevent further loss of life was urgently needed and so the Thames Barrier was built in 1984 to protect London. It is the world's largest movable flood barrier, spanning 520 metres (1706 feet) and consists of ten separate, movable steel gates. When raised, the main gates stand as high as a five-storey building. There is a model of the barrier inside the centre, along with an interesting exhibition and spectacular audio-visual shows which explain its history, construction and operation.

⊖ New Cross, New Cross Gate

🚆 Charlton, then shuttle service

〰️ regular services from Westminster Pier (75 minutes) and Greenwich (25 minutes); a round barrier boat cruise (0181 305 0300) runs from Barrier Gardens Pier, with full commentary on the Barrier and local geography (30 minutes)

♿

Exhibition Open: Monday–Friday, 10.00 a.m.–5.00 p.m.; Saturday and Sunday, 10.30 a.m.–5.30 p.m.

£

London Bridge

London Bridge was the only crossing over the lower Thames until 1750, when Westminster Bridge was opened. Originally constructed by the Romans, it has been rebuilt several times and the present one dates from 1973. The previous one was sold for £1m and is now a tourist attraction in Arizona in the USA. The story goes that the owner thought London Bridge was Tower Bridge and therefore bought the wrong one, although he claims he had always intended to buy London Bridge!

RIVER TRIPS AND SIGHTSEEING TOURS

Numerous cruise boats take tours up and down the river and are reasonably priced. Frequency depends on the time of year. For recorded information on river trips phone the London Tourist Board on 0891 505471 or contact the piers direct on the phone numbers given below:

Catamaran Cruisers

Charing Cross Pier, Victoria Embankment, WC2 (0171 839 3572)
To Greenwich and the Tower of London, also evening cruises.
Θ Embankment
🚌 9, 11, 23, 24, 29
£–££

Tower Pier

Tower Hill, EC3 (0171 488 0344)
Regular service to Westminster and Greenwich, with a frequent ferry to HMS *Belfast*.
Θ Tower Hill
🚌 15, 42, 78, 100
£–££

Westminster Pier

Victoria Embankment, SW1 (0171 930 3373)
Downstream to Canary Wharf, Greenwich and the Thames Barrier. Upstream to Hampton Court, Kew, Putney and Richmond. Also circular cruises and evening and lunch cruises.
Θ Westminster
🚌 3, 12, 53, 77A, 109
£–££

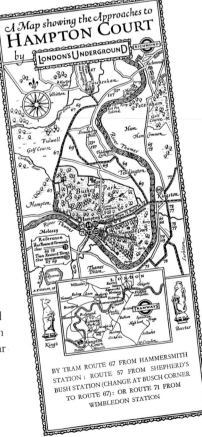

A Map showing the Approaches to HAMPTON COURT by LONDON'S UNDERGROUND

BY TRAM ROUTE 67 FROM HAMMERSMITH STATION : ROUTE 57 FROM SHEPHERD'S BUSH STATION (CHANGE AT BUSCH CORNER TO ROUTE 67): OR ROUTE 71 FROM WIMBLEDON STATION

LONDON'S CANALS

The Grand Union, Regent's and Hertford Canals swing in a wide arc through the heart of London to link with the River Lea Navigation to the east and the River Thames to the south, and with another arm dropping south to Brentford, where it joins the Thames too. Today the whole canal system in London is generally known as the Grand Union Canal; weaving between factories and warehouses or opening into parks, gardens and nature reserves, it is a fascinating place to explore.

The Maida Hill tunnel, under Edgware Road, is a 'legging' tunnel through which there is no towing path. Spoil from the tunnel excavation was laid on the field of a nearby landowner, Thomas Lord. The field was later to become the world-famous cricket ground.

Now known as 'Blow-up Bridge', Macclesfield Bridge in Regent's Park was the scene of an explosion in 1874 when a barge carrying a cargo of gunpowder ignited as it was passing under it. The original bridge columns were used to rebuild the bridge but they were placed the wrong way round, so the marks worn by the towing ropes are today on the wrong side.

See pages 117–18 for details of various canal trips.

INDOOR FUN AND LEARNING

INDOOR ACTIVITIES

W ET weather need never be a problem in London as there is an incredible wealth of indoor activities for children to do. If they want to let off steam, the latest trend to hit London are indoor adventure playgrounds, packed with all sorts of imaginative equipment, such as ball ponds, tunnels and towers. Staff at these popular activity centres will supervise the children, leaving the adults free to watch or have a peaceful cup of coffee. Another top attraction is the Pepsi Trocadero, which is packed with the latest hi-tech games.

Many of London's best museums, galleries and arts centres organize excellent and creative workshops catering to a wide range of interests. Young drama buffs can tread the boards at children's theatres or choose from a number of drama courses. There is also a lively tradition of musical activities for children from ballet and dance classes to playing in an orchestra and singing in a choir, as well as specially arranged concerts.

FUN AND GAMES

INDOOR ADVENTURE PLAYGROUNDS

Action Station

Pavilion Building, Lakeside Shopping Centre, West Thurrock, Grays, Essex (01708 868222: recorded information)
This adventure playground is a little way out of London, just east of the M25, but has to be included here as it is probably one of the best in Britain. It has the highest indoor slide in the country and five themed areas, including 'Trash Can Alley', the 'Swamp' and the 'Crazy Maze'.

Birthday parties can be held here, with goody bags provided for a charge, and there is a good café.

🚇 Chafford, then bus

♿

🅿 free at the Lakeside Shopping Centre

Open: Monday–Friday, 11.00 a.m.–8.00 p.m.; Saturday, 10.00 a.m.–7.30 p.m.; Sunday, 11.00 a.m.–6.00 p.m.

£–££ for children, free for adults

Discovery Zone

The Junction Shopping Centre, Clapham Junction, SW11 (0171 223 1717)
See also page 186
Suitable for children up to twelve, the equipment here includes a rollerslide maze (you go up a ball staircase, through a tunnel maze and down the rollerslide), an obstacle course, a ball pond, a 'Moonwalk Bounce' and a 'Mountain Climb' – climb up the mountain without touching the balls.

There is also an over-eights club where children aged up to twelve are supervised, leaving parents free. For under-fives there are 'Jumpin' Jives' – active, stimulating classes that help to improve co-ordination.

🚇 Clapham Junction
🚌 35, 77A, 156, 295, 344
Limited ♿ (phone in advance)
Open: daily, 10.00 a.m.–8.00 p.m.
£ for children, free for adults

Fantasy Island

Vale Farm, Watford Road, Wembley, Middlesex (0181 904 9044)
Based on a jungle theme, the main playground comprises a three-storey tower of rope bridges, swirling slides, secret tunnels, ball ponds and bouncy rubber logs that squeak such phrases as 'What a wallop!' when activated. For toddlers there is a smaller-scale jungle with simpler equipment.

Plenty of refreshment facilities for children including a large self-service café. Visit Fantasy Island during the week and your kids eat for 1p when you order lunch.

⊖ North Wembley
🚌 182, 245
♿
Open: daily, 10.00 a.m.–4.30 p.m. (phone on weekdays as times may change)
£ for children, free for adults

The House of Fun

The Bridge Leisure Centre, Kangley Bridge Road, Lower Sydenham, SE26 (0181 659 9400)
This playground is great for younger children, with plenty to jump and slide on, but perhaps a little limited for more demanding, older children. There is now a café for refreshments.

🚇 Lower Sydenham
🚌 352 (Monday–Saturday)
♿
Open: daily, 10.00 a.m.–6.00 p.m.
£ for children, free for adults

Krazy Kids

213 Mile End Road, Stepney Green, E1 (0171 790 4000)
This playground has a multi-level structure with a jungle theme which appeals to children. Refreshment facilities are limited.
⊖ Stepney Green
🚌 25
Limited ♿
Open: daily, 10.00 a.m.–7.00 p.m.
£ for children, free for adults

Monkey Business

222 Green Lanes, Palmers Green, N13 (0181 886 7520) (entrance via Lodge Drive behind Iceland)
Monkeys are the theme here and children can 'monkey around' a tree house, Tarzan ropes, ball ponds (right), a tube slide and a maze. There is also a special toddlers' area, a 'haunted' spook room and a café.
⊖ Manor House
🚆 Palmers Green and Southgate
🚌 141, 171A
P
♿
Open: daily, 10.00 a.m.–7.00 p.m.
£ for children, free for adults

Pirates Playhouse

Sobell Sports Centre, Hornsey Road, Holloway, N7 (0171 609 2166)
This playground has three levels and includes slides, punch bags and bridges – all with a pirate theme. Adults can accompany children so long as the playground does not get too crowded and there is a separate space for toddlers. This section is quieter and has simpler equipment, such as a ball pond and bouncy corner.
Entry price depends on height – it's cheaper if a child is under 1 metre (3 feet 3 inches) tall. The maximum height for entry is 1.39 metres (4 feet 7 inches).
⊖ Finsbury Park, Holloway Road
🚆 Finsbury Park
🚌 43, 271
No ♿
Open: Monday–Friday, 9.00 a.m.–6.00 p.m.; Saturday and Sunday, 9.30 a.m.–7.00 p.m.
£ for children, free for adults

The Playhouse

The Old Gymnasium, Highbury Grove School, Highbury New Park, N6 (0171 704 9424)
No children over 1.49 metres (4 feet 11 inches) are allowed in, and under-fives have their own play area. Birthday parties can be held here – there are catering facilities.

⊖ Highbury & Islington
🚆 Canonbury, Highbury & Islington
🚌 236
♿

Open: daily, 10.00 a.m.–7.00 p.m.
£ for children, free for adults

Snakes & Ladders

Syon Park, Brentford, Middlesex (0181 847 0946)
Located within the grounds of Syon House, Snakes & Ladders offers go-karting as well as a huge multi-level play area. There is also a refreshment area.

⊖ Gunnersbury, then bus
🚆 Brentford
🚌 116, 117, 237, 267
♿

Open: daily, 10.00 a.m.–4.15 p.m. (last admission)
£ for children, free for adults

Tiger's Eye

42 Station Road, Mitcham, SW19 (0181 543 1655)
There is a large multi-level play area with slides and a tunnel, a 'haunted house' and a go-karting course. Birthday parties can be held here too. Refreshment facilities are available.

⊖ Colliers Wood
🚌 57, 152, 155, 200
♿

Open: daily, 10.00 a.m.–7.00 p.m.
£ for children, free for adults

GAMES CENTRES

Pepsi Trocadero

Piccadilly Circus, WC1 (0990 100456: information hotline)
Originally a hotel, the Trocadero has been given a revitalizing facelift and is now London's premier entertainment centre, with themed restaurants, shops and games and rides. There are seven floors of visually explosive attractions, including the most up-to-date virtual reality adventures, simulation rides and interactive games.

Entrance to the complex is free, with individual charges for each attraction. Look out for special offers, giving discounts for rides. Some activities are suitable for wheelchair users – see individual entries on the following pages.

⊖ Leicester Square, Piccadilly Circus
🚌 3, 12, 14, 19, 22, 38

Open: daily, 10.00 a.m.– midnight; Friday and Saturday, 10.00 a.m.– 1.00 a.m.

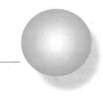

The Emaginator

This sensational ride-cinema with moving seats brings a whole new dimension to movie-going. The cinema screens specially made action-adventure films which demonstrate the full range of simulation hydraulics. Titles include 'Cosmic Pinball', where you are the ball, and 'Space Race', where you hurtle through space on a special mission.

&

£–££

Funland and Lazerbowl

A huge and noisy amusement centre, packed with all the latest computer games, as well as virtual reality simulators and children's rides. Lazerbowl is a futuristic bowling game where the pins are actually only lazers.

&

£–££

The Giant Drop

The only indoor free-fall ride in the world. If you can stomach it, you will be hauled up to 40 metres (125 feet), then hurtle to the ground through a haze of neon lights and electronic sounds.

Limited &

£–££

Trocadero

Pepsi IMAX® 3D Cinema

This cinema shows amazing 2D and 3D movies on a screen five storeys high. The audience wears headsets with 'surround sound' to heighten the virtual reality experience.

&

£–££

The Rainforest Café

Take a walk on the wild side amid the flora and fauna normally only found in the Brazilian rainforest. Here you will be taken on a virtual safari and come face to face with tropical fish, elephants and gorillas!

&

£

Segaworld

Take a futuristic journey up one of Europe's longest escalators and into six floors of high-tech adventure. Here you will find some of the world's best ride attractions and you can experience anything from an underwater world with the '3D Terrors of the Deep', to the fun of the fair on the 'Magic of the Carnival Ride'.

No &

£ entry, £ for each ride

Virtual Glider

Your mission: to launch off the top of a building into a futuristic city or glide around the spectacular rock formations of the Grand Canyon – and try to land safely. First used for military training in the United States, this interactive hang-gliding experience will really test your skills.

No &

£

Virtuality

A selection of virtual reality games where you will be transported to other worlds.

&

£

ARTS CENTRES, GALLERIES, MUSEUMS AND THEATRES

The following venues, listed in geographical area for easier reference, hold regular workshops for children, featuring a great variety of activities. Phone for information on current events.

CENTRAL

London Transport Museum

The Piazza, Covent Garden, WC2 (0171 379 6344)

See also page 66

The museum offers a full programme of activities and events from storytelling to children's workshops. The Wheelie Club, a club for five- to twelve-year-olds, entitles members to free admission to the museum plus a host of special activities.

Θ Covent Garden

🚍 6, 9, 11, 15, 23

♿

Open: daily, 10.00 a.m.–6.00 p.m. (Friday, from 11.00 a.m); last admission 5.15 p.m.

£ (under-fives free)

National Gallery

Trafalgar Square, WC1 (0171 747 2885: recorded information)
See also page 76
For selected exhibitions there are light-hearted quizzes and competitions suitable for ages twelve and under.

Θ Charing Cross, Leicester Square

🚍 9, 11, 23, 24, 29

♿

Open: Monday–Saturday, 10.00 a.m.–6.00 p.m. (Wednesday, to 8.00 p.m.); Sunday, 12 noon–6.00 p.m. (closed 1 January, Good Friday, May Day holiday and 24–26 December)
Free

Tate Gallery

Millbank, SW1 (0171 887 8000; 0171 887 8008: recorded information)
See also page 78
There is an extensive programme of activities during all three school holidays for children of all ages – phone for a leaflet.

A new innovation is the Art Trolley. Aimed specifically at enabling children to get more from the Tate, the trolley can be found at different sites within the gallery each Sunday afternoon between 2.15 p.m. and 4.45 p.m. It is staffed by one of the Tate's education officers who organizes various paper-based activities (such as drawing or collage-making) for children to join in. Kids can borrow all the equipment they need from the trolley and participation is free.

Θ Pimlico

🚍 2, C10, 36, 77A, 88

♿

Open: daily, 10.00 a.m.–5.50 p.m. (Sunday, from 2.00 p.m.)
Free (£ for special exhibitions)

Unicorn Arts Theatre

6 Great Newport Street, WC2 (0171 836 3334: box office)
See also pages 145 and 186

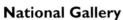

In addition to its excellent professional performances for children, the Unicornalso holds plenty of theatre-based activities for children to participate in. Half-term and holiday workshops include Performance Specials, which are short drama courses which work towards a performance for parents.

During term-time the Monday Club offers drama training for eight- to twelve year-olds, while Unicorn Plus, a performance-based group, is for older children (twelve- to sixteen-year-olds).

The theatre also holds open days, when visitors can take part in an afternoon of free workshops, chats with actors and face-painting.

An excellent way to get the most out of the Unicorn is to become a family member, whereby you can get discounts on tickets for shows and workshops.

⊖ Leicester Square
🚌 24, 29, 176
No ♿
£–££

Wallace Collection

Hertford House, Manchester Square, W1 (0171 935 0687)
Although the elegant surroundings of Hertford House, with its sophisticated collections of Sèvres porcelain, paintings, furniture and clocks, do not at first seem particularly children-friendly, in fact the Wallace Collection has a very good reputation for its imaginative and creative family events. Activities include mobile hanging and making Christmas cards – using stencils, templates, collage and colouring inspired by works in the gallery – and are suitable for children aged from six to twelve (book in advance).

⊖ Bond Street, Marble Arch
🚌 2, 30, 74, 113, 139
♿

Open: Monday–Saturday, 10.00 a.m.–5.00 p.m.; Sunday, 2.00 p.m.–5.00 p.m. (closed 24–26 December and 1 January)
Free

EAST

Barbican Centre

Silk Street, EC2 (0171 638 8891: box office)
See also pages 146
The Barbican's Splodge Club for five- to twelve-year-olds offers a wealth of activities for children to enjoy and participate in. Entertainment includes story-telling at the children's library on one Saturday each month between 11.00 a.m. and 12 noon for five-year-olds and upwards, film shows every Saturday and occasional concerts.

Creative workshops are held in conjunction with festivals and special events. A particular highlight is the annual week-long Summer in the City Festival for children aged two to eight. Held during the summer holidays, the Splodge Club organizes five days of games, activities, competitions, theatre and puppet shows, and workshops.

There is a small membership fee for joining the Splodge Club. Members receive a mailing every 2 months with a leaflet and details of special offers. The club also organizes parties with clowns and entertainers several times a year.

⊖ Barbican

🚌 4 (Monday–Saturday), 56

♿

Open: Centre: daily, 10.00 a.m.–11.00 p.m.

£–££

Bethnal Green Museum of Childhood

Cambridge Heath Road, E2 (0181 980 2415: recorded information)
See also page 74
Workshops lasting 1¾ hours are held for children aged three and over from 11.00 a.m. and 2.00 p.m. on Saturday. These cover a variety of creative activities, such as painting, drawing, making models and masks. It is not necessary to book a place – you can just drop in when visiting this ever-popular museum.

⊖ Bethnal Green

🚌 8

Limited ♿

Open: Monday–Thursday and Saturday, 10.00 a.m.–5.50 p.m.; Sunday, 2.30 p.m.–5.50 p.m.

Free

Geffrye Museum

Kingsland Road, Shoreditch, E2 (0171 739 9893; 0171 739 8543: recorded information)
The Geffrye Museum is a unique establishment, managing to combine its important collection on the history of the English domestic interior with an intimate and friendly atmosphere, making it a family favourite. To complement these regular special exhibitions, there are some excellent workshops both for children and adults (children under eight must be accompanied by an adult). Held at half-terms, holidays and on most Saturdays, a wide range of imaginative activities give children a chance to explore how people lived in the past, as well have fun learning such diverse new skills as making wigs, designing textiles or making pottery Josiah Wedgwood-style. Phone for details of current programme.

The Geffrye has also earned a high reputation for its educational services, winning a prestigious award for its imaginative work in this field.

⊖ Old Street

🚆 Dalston Kingsland, Liverpool Street

🚌 22A, 22B, 67, 149, 243 (Monday–Saturday)

♿

Open: Tuesday–Saturday, 10.00 a.m.–5.00 p.m. Sunday and bank holiday Monday, 2.00 p.m–5.00 p.m.

Holiday activities are free for all ages; a small charge is made occasionally for special events

A children's workshop at the Geffrye Museum

<u>NORTH</u>

Camden Arts Centre

Arkwright Road (corner of Finchley Road), NW3 (0171 435 2643)

The centre offers a range of daytime, evening and weekend classes for children and adults, including ceramics, painting, drawing and sculpture. Classes are run by practising artists. During the summer holidays there are special projects for children, including courses in claywork and mixed media.

⊖ Finchley Road

🚇 Finchley Road & Frognal

🚌 13, 46, 82, 113

No ⅙

Open: Tuesday–Thursday, 11.00 a.m.–7.00 p.m.; Friday–Sunday, 11.00 a.m.–5.30 p.m.

£

Jacksons Lane Community Centre

269a Archway Road, N6 (0181 341 4421: box office)

Jacksons Lane offers a variety of circus workshops. For children aged five to eight there is a circus skills class each Wednesday at 5.00 p.m. (during term-time), where they can learn such skills as juggling, low tightrope-walking and plate-spinning. For over-eights there are 6-week courses in trapeze and web rope skills. Additional workshops are held during half-terms, but there are no classes during the holidays.

Jacksons Lane also holds a lively drama club for eleven- to sixteen-year-olds on Saturday mornings. Children work towards productions by the award-winning Jacksons Lane Youth Theatre Company.

Highgate After Schools Club offers activities, crafts and general fun for five- to eleven-year-olds after school every day. Activities include cookery, art, table tennis, board games, and storytime. There is also a quiet space for doing homework. Children must be registered at least one day in advance (phone 0181 341 4590/0181 340 5226 for details).

For younger children (aged two to eight) Crazee Kids arts courses offer a chance to explore creative movement, dance, drama and music through stimulating activities and games. Percussion, songs and rhymes offer understanding of rhythm and music, and balls, hoops and toys provide movement, dance and drama opportunities. Class times vary, so phone 0181 444 5333 for details.

⊖ Highgate

🚌 43, 134, 263

♿

Open: Centre: daily, 10.00 a.m.–11.00 p.m.

£

Old Bull Arts Centre

68 High Street, Barnet, Herts (0181 449 0048)

Term-time courses in drama and dance are held for children aged from eighteen months to sixteen. The youngest children go to a Parent and Toddler dance group, progressing to a Creative Dance class for three- to five-year-olds and a drama club for eight- to eleven-year-olds. The oldest group (twelve- to sixteen-year-olds) can join the youth theatre which puts on about two performances a year.

At half-terms there is a range of varied workshops and one-day drama courses, while in the summer holidays drama summer schools are usually held for two age groups (nine- to twelve-year-olds and thirteen- to sixteen-year-olds), where children learn about all aspects of the theatre, from stage management to lighting.

Another exciting and popular course for children is Kathak, a northern Indian style of dance. Classes are suitable for children aged six to sixteen.

⊖ High Barnet

🚆 New Barnet

🚌 34, 107, 184, 234, 263

♿

Open: Tuesday–Friday, 10.00 a.m.–5.30 p.m., unless there is a show on, in which case the box office is open until 9.00 p.m.; Saturday and Sunday, 1.00 p.m.–9.00 p.m.

£

Tricycle Theatre

269 Kilburn High Road, NW6 (0171 328 1000)

See also page 144

More than 250 theatre-based workshops are held throughout the year for children aged eighteen months to sixteen and are nearly always over-subscribed. For younger children the emphasis is on fun, and classes comprise movement, singing and clapping. As children get older, the classes become more structured, with such themes as circus skills, mime and puppet-making. During half-term, Easter and summer holidays there are also short drama courses which often culminate in performances for parents and friends.

⊖ Kilburn

🚆 Brondesbury

🚌 16, 16A, 32

♿

£–££

Battersea Arts Centre

Old Town Hall, Lavender Hill, SW11 (0171 223 6557)
See also page 60
Based a hop, skip and a jump from Clapham Junction station, BAC (Battersea Arts Centre) has a packed programme of activities for anyone aged two to twenty-five. Holiday workshops and special events are held throughout the year.

Drama also features strongly at BAC. The Acting Factory of weekly after-school classes is available for children aged five to fifteen. Courses run over an academic year, although it is possible to join for one term at a time. The main aim of the classes is to allow children to express themselves, achieved through role-playing games and improvisations. At the end of each term children present a performance to their parents.

If you don't want the commitment of a whole term's course, then a half-term workshop may be more suitable (available at the autumn and spring half-terms only). The workshops last for about a couple of hours each day and are based on a variety of themes, including puppetry and story-telling.

🚇 Clapham Junction
🚌 39, 77, 77A
♿

Open: daily, 10.00 a.m.–9.00 p.m. (Monday, to 6.00 p.m.)
£–££

Dulwich Picture Gallery

College Road, Dulwich, SE21 (0181 693 5254)
See also page 76
This attractive gallery holds regular holiday activities linked to temporary exhibitions as well as the permanent collection. Dry media only are used inside the gallery for obvious reasons, but other activities such as making collages take place in the nearby vestry in the winter and in the garden in the summer. Highlights of a recent summer season of flower-related workshops included 'Design a flower power T-shirt', 'Make a bug badge' and 'Create a miniature garden'.

For older children the excellent 'Summer sketchbook course' is an ideal opportunity to develop a portfolio before going on to study art at A-level standard.

All activities are organized at fairly short notice, so phone for details.

🚇 Herne Hill, North Dulwich, West Dulwich
🚌 P4
♿

Open: Tuesday–Saturday, 10.00 a.m.–5.00 p.m.; Saturday, from 11.00 a.m.; Sunday, 2.00 p.m.–5.00 p.m.
£ (free on Friday and for children under sixteen)

Imperial War Museum

Lambeth Road, SE1 (0171 416 5000; 0171 820 1683: recorded information)
See also page 70
Various holiday and half-term events including some art activities are held here to

tie in with some current exhibitions. Role-playing workshops are particularly successful – during a recent exhibition on espionage, children had the opportunity of pretending to be wartime spies, following a special gallery trail. Other role-playing games have included pretending to be war reporters. Children have also been taught how to camouflage themselves.

There are also colouring-in sheets relating to exhibitions and an annual Easter Egg hunt with free chocolate mini eggs for all those who complete the hunt successfully.

⊖ Elephant & Castle, Lambeth North
🚋 Waterloo
🚌 C10, 12, 53, 68, 344
♿ (please phone 0171 416 5320 giving 48 hours' notice if possible)
Open: daily, 10.00 a.m.–6.00 p.m.
£ (free after 4.30 p.m.)

Museum of the Moving Image (MOMI)

South Bank, Waterloo, SE1 (0171 401 2636: recorded information)
See also page 60
Workshops relating to the whole history of the moving image from puppet-making courses to an introduction to the multi-media culture are on offer here at half-terms and holidays. Recent events include a hands-on television workshop that gave children the opportunity to 'make' a TV commercial.

Some activities are not suitable for younger children, so phone first. It is also wise to book a place in advance, although some workshops allow people to drop in during their visit to the museum.

⊖/🚋 Waterloo
🚌 68, 168, 171, 176, 188
♿ (phone 0171 815 1350 for more details)
Open: daily except 24–26 December, 10.00 a.m.–6.00 p.m. (last admission 5.00 p.m.)
£

Polka Theatre

240 The Broadway, Wimbledon, SW19 (0181 543 4888)
See also page 144
For very young thespians there is a 'music for under-threes' club, meeting weekly on Thursday mornings and comprising movement, music games and stories. There are weekly drama groups for six- to eight-year-olds and nine- to twelve-year-olds, as well as three-day half-term courses in music and drama for three- to five-year-olds. In addition, there is a weekly Junior Youth Theatre for thirteen- to sixteen-year-olds.

⊖/🚋Wimbledon
🚌 57, 93, 155
Limited ♿
£–££

Royal Festival Hall

South Bank, SE1 (0171 960 4242: box office)

Although the free foyer musical events and some of the exhibitions held on the South Bank appeal to all ages, the Royal Festival Hall also holds several events specially for children. The Great Outdoor Festival of Performing Arts is held every summer and includes children's shows, and the National Festival of Music for Youth takes place every July, when school orchestras, jazz and pop bands from all over Britain descend on the South Bank for a musical bonanza.

Another regular highlight is the Blitz, a festival of dance with performances and workshops that children (and adults) can participate in. The education department also organizes regular one-off activities, such as percussion workshops, which are mostly held at weekends. Phone for information on forthcoming events.

θ /🖵 Waterloo

🚌 P11, 68, 77, 171, 188

♿

Open: daily, 10.00 a.m.–10.00 p.m.

££

WEST

Carousel

Flat 1, 614 Fulham Road, SW6 (0171 731 7921)

Holiday and half-term activities are offered for children aged three to ten in drama, art, music, indoor and outdoor games at the Brompton Oratory.

θ South Kensington

🚌 14, 345

No ♿

££

London Toy and Model Museum

21–23 Craven Hill, Bayswater, W2 (0171 402 5222: recorded information)
See also page 75
The emphasis for activities here is on fun rather than learning. Highlights are seasonal events such as a Christmas Grotto, a Halloween ghost train and traditional fairground games, as well as weekend quizzes, marble championships, face-painting and a chance to try out the latest toys from Hamley's.
⊖ Bayswater, Queensway
🚌 12, 94
Limited ♿
Open: Monday–Saturday, 10.00 a.m.–5.30 p.m. (Sunday and bank holiday Monday, from 11.00 a.m.); last admission 4.30 p.m.
£ (free for under-fours)

The Natural History Museum

Cromwell Road, South Kensington, SW7 (0171 938 9123)
See also page 55
Half-term and holiday activities linked with popular galleries (such as the Dinosaur exhibition) are regularly held. Typical activities include fossil-finding, trails, quizzes and crafts with a natural history link such as paper-making. Entrance to the workshops is free upon entry to the museum, and you should book in advance.
⊖ South Kensington
🚌 C1, 9, 14, 52, 74
♿
Open: Monday–Saturday, 10.00 a.m.–5.50 p.m.; Sunday, 11.00 a.m.–5.50 p.m. (closed 23–26 December)
£ (free after 4.30 p.m. on weekdays and after 5.00 p.m. on Saturday and Sunday; under-fives are free always)

Science Museum

Exhibition Road, South Kensington, SW7 (0171 938 8080; 0171 938 8008: recorded information)
See also page 56
The museum holds great half-term and holiday activities, suitable for children aged six and upwards. These events include treasure hunt trails, drama presentations where children can participate in a performance linked to a particular gallery and art workshops. Activities are free on entry to the museum but must be booked in advance.

Equally popular (especially as a party treat) are Science Nights. Small groups of eight- to eleven-year-olds can spend the night at the Science Museum (under supervision) and enjoy a packed programme of activities, talks, trails and competitions (plus some sleep!). Phone 0171 938 9785 for more details.
⊖ South Kensington
🚌 C1, 9, 14, 52, 74
♿

Properties of water are explained in 'The Garden' at the Science Museum (see page 56)

Open: daily, 10.00 a.m.–6.00 p.m.
£ (free after 4.30 p.m.; under-fives are free always)

Waterman's Arts Centre

40 High Street, Brentford, Middlesex (0181 568 1176: box office)
See also page 145
Pre-school children can enjoy 'Pandemonium', music sessions that are held in the foyer each Wednesday morning (threes to fours at 10.00 a.m., under-twos at 10.50 a.m. and twos at 11.45 a.m.). Booking in advance is not necessary.
🚇 Brentford, Kew Bridge
🚌 65, 116, 117, 237, 267
♿

Open: Tuesday–Sunday, 9.00 a.m.–11.00 p.m. approx. (depending on shows taking place)
£

Cookery Classes

For would-be Raymond Blancs and Anton Mosimanns, the cookery classes at the Cordon Bleu Culinary Institute, 114 Marylebone Lane, W1 (0171 935 3503) are a fun way of learning basic culinary skills.

Beginners can start with a series of ten workshops held on Saturday mornings, while for the more advanced there are five-day workshops in the holidays. Classes are suitable for children aged seven to fourteen and you will need to book in advance.
⊖ Bond Street
🚌 2, 7, 8, 13, 98
No ♿

Brass rubbing

The following brass rubbing centres provide everything you will need to learn how to make rubbings of historical brasses. The cost of rubbing is graded according to the size of the brass.

All Hallows-by-the-Tower

Byward Street, EC3 (0171 481 2928)

An important collection of brasses includes a Resurrection brass, one of only three in the country. Other subjects include knights and animals.

⊖ Tower Hill

🚌 15, 100

No ♿

Open: daily, 10.00 a.m.–4.30 p.m. (Sunday, from 1.00 p.m.)

London Brass Rubbing Centre

St Martin-in-the-Fields

WC2 (0171 930 9306)

Over 100 different brasses can be found here in the crypt, including dragons, elephants, griffins, Celtic designs and knights and ladies.

⊖ Charing Cross, Embankment

🚉 Charing Cross

🚌 9, 11, 24, 29, 176

No ♿

Open: daily, 10.00 a.m.–6.00 p.m. (Sunday, from 12.00 noon)

£

Westminster Abbey

Broad Sanctuary, SW1 (0171 222 2085)

The brass rubbing centre in the cloisters of Westminster Abbey contains a wonderful selection of brasses from around the country, including historical figures, St George and the Dragon and contemporary pieces.

⊖ Westminster

🚌 11, 12, 24, 88, 211

Open: Monday–Saturday, 9.00 a.m.–5.00 p.m.

£

BALLET AND DANCE SCHOOLS

Chelsea Ballet School

6 Upper Cheyne Row, SW3 (0171 351 4117)

A range of dance classes from modern and tap to traditional classical ballet for children and adults of all abilities are held here, taught by leading professional teachers. Children need to commit themselves to a full term's course, and, although the classes can be taken for fun, natural talent will be developed to professional standards.

The school also has branches at Dulwich, Sloane Square and Knightsbridge.

⊖ Sloane Square, then bus

🚌 11, 19, 22, 49, 211

No ♿

££

Southwest Ballet School

474 Upper Richmond Road, Putney, SW15 (0181 878 9486)

The school holds classes in ballet and tap dancing in Putney, Battersea, Hammersmith and Wimbledon Park, for children who enjoy dance for fun or for those wishing to take examinations. Uniform is also available from the school if required. A free trial lesson is offered but classes have to be booked for a term at a time.

🚊 Putney

⊖ East Putney

🚌 74, 337

No ♿

££

The Spring School of Ballet

The Contact Centre, Hambalt Road, Clapham SW4 (0181 673 2963)

Saturday classes and after-school classes in ballet and tap dancing are offered, with the emphasis on enjoyment (although there is the option to take Royal Academy of Dancing exams). Booking in advance is recommended, and classes last for a term.

Θ Clapham Common, Clapham South

🚌 60, 155

No ♿

££

DRAMA SCHOOLS AND COURSES

Children don't need to commit themselves to a full-time drama school to be able to learn the skills of the stage in London. Many drama schools and theatre groups run after-school courses.

A Class Act

3 Lainson Street, Southfields, SW18 (0181 870 0466)

Drama can be an excellent way of helping children overcome shyness, and A Class Act drama group strives to this end, encouraging children to enjoy using their imagination and contributing to a session held in local venues. Younger children (aged three to four) use games and songs as the basis for their performances, while older children (aged five to seven) concentrate on drama, parents sometimes dropping in to watch them perform at the end of a session.

Θ Southfields

🚌 39, 156

No ♿

££

Anna Scher Children's Theatre

70–71 Barnsbury Road, Islington, N1 (0171 278 2101)

After-school classes are available for children aged six years and upwards for this highly popular drama school (Pauline Quirke and Linda Robson from 'Birds of a Feather' are among its most successful alumni). There is also a summer school.

Θ Angel, then bus 153 (Monday–Saturday)

🚌 30, 73

No ♿

££

The Arts Educational London Schools

Cone Ripman House, 14 Bath Road, Chiswick, W4 (0181 994 9366)

One of the leading centres for arts education, this school provides tuition in all dance forms – ballet, tap, modern, jazz and ballroom – as well as musical theatre, violin, guitar, singing, drama, computer studies, art and exercise. Children aged three and over are welcome, and classes are held on weekday evenings and Saturdays. A special feature is the Summer Dance School and Music Workshops held during the summer holidays.

⊖ Stamford Brook, Turnham Green

🚌 E3, 94

No ♿

££

MUSIC SCHOOLS, COURSES AND CHOIRS

Baylis Programme

English National Opera, London Coliseum, St Martin's Lane, WC2 (0171 729 8550)

The programme is an educational incentive of the English National Opera which aims to introduce as many people (both adults and children) as possible to opera. Family Days, practical workshops, are held where children and parents can explore drama and music together. There are also two youth opera groups during term-time: 'Live Wires' for eight- to twelve-year-olds and 'Live Culture' for twelve- to sixteen-year-olds.

⊖ Leicester Square

🚌 24, 29, 68, 91, 168, 176

Limited ♿

Open: times vary (phone in advance)

£–££

Bea's Baby Music School

102 Bramfield Road, SW11 (0171 228 0904)

Teacher Bea Couch offers a boisterous range of musical activities for young children (from six months to five years), featuring traditional nursery rhymes, modern children's songs and hands-on instrumental sessions in different venues. Phone for details. Although children can attend individual sessions, you are advised to book for a term.

🚉 Clapham Junction

🚌 49, 337

♿ (some venues)

£–££

The Guildhall School of Music and Drama

Silk Street, Barbican, EC2 (0171 638 1770: junior department)

Music courses for all abilities are offered here on Saturdays during term-time. Younger children (aged five to eight) interested in learning a stringed instrument can enrol on a five-week preparatory course, at the end of which they can join the beginner string-training course. There are also two orchestras that children can join.

For musically gifted children aged from eight to eighteen the best course of action is to join the Junior School, which also holds its classes on a Saturday. If you pass the audition, you will receive individual tuition, as well as group ensemble and orchestral training.

⊖ Barbican
🚌 4 (Monday–Saturday), 56
♿
££

Monkey Music

8 Idmiston Road, West Norwood, SE27 (0181 761 7271)
Established at fourteen venues across London, Monkey Music teaches music and music-making to babies and young children. Each session is run by a qualified and experienced children's music specialist with children grouped in small classes according to their ages (from six months to five years). Activities include action songs and rhymes, musical games, storytelling with instrumental accompaniment and playing percussion instruments. Phone for information on venues.
♿ (most venues)
££

New London Children's Choir

Secretary: 41 Abedare Gardens, NW6 (0181 444 3110: information)
The choir rehearses every Sunday at its base in Highgate and performs regularly all over London. The choir covers a wide repertoire, including several modern pieces. It is recommended that children should be able to sight-read before applying to join the senior choir. There is a training choir for eight- to eleven-year-olds, the senior choir for eleven- to eighteen-year-olds (entrance by audition), a 'fun' youth choir and a barbershop group.

In recent years the choir has made several recordings (including Tchaikovsky's 'Nutcracker') and has commissioned new works.
⊖ Highgate
🚌 43, 134, 263
No ♿
££

Tafelmusik

Tempo House, 15 Falcon Road, SW11 (0171 978 7060)
With several branches across London (phone for details), Tafelmusik is a German-based programme of creative and lively workshops for children from eight months to eight years. Each workshop lasts 45 minutes and involves dancing, singing, and playing instruments. Older children also learn about the theory of music.

It is necessary to book in advance for a 12-week term, although it is possible to pay for one trial lesson.
££

CHAPTER THREE

CENTRES OF DISCOVERY

TODAY, museums and galleries have shaken off their stuffy image and are exciting centres of discovery for children. The major museums in London are the British Museum, which traces the history of the world through its art and culture, and the South Kensington museums, comprising the Natural History Museum, the Science Museum and the Victoria & Albert Museum, with its wonderful collection of decorative arts.

Greenwich is a wonderful place to spend a day. You can board a tea clipper (*Cutty Sark*, page 69), get your hands on a missile-control system at the National Maritime Museum (page 71) and even stand astride two time zones.

The best galleries for children include the National Gallery, the National Portrait Gallery and The Tate, which have some of the most important pictures in the world. Some of the smaller venues also work hard at getting children actively involved as a means of improving their understanding and appreciation of art in general (see pages 76–9).

London White Card

The London White Card is a three- or seven-day pass for many of the better-known museums and galleries. The price varies depending on whether you buy a card for an individual or a family (two adults and two children). It is excellent value, and it can save you money if you go to lots of places and if you wish to visit the same place several times. The card is available at the following participating venues and at Tourist and Travel Centres: Barbican Art Gallery; Courtauld Institute; Design Museum;. Hayward Gallery; Imperial War Museum; London Transport Museum; Museum of London; Museum of the Moving Image (MOMI); National Maritime Museum, Old Royal Observatory and Queen's House; Natural History Museum; Royal Academy of Arts; Science Museum; and the Victoria & Albert Museum (except certain tempo-rary exhibitions).

❖

MAJOR MUSEUMS

British Museum

Great Russell Street, WC1 (0171 636 1555)

One of the greatest landmarks in London, the imposing buildings of the British Museum are home to the country's finest cultural treasures. The museum is always busy, so it is a good idea to plan in advance what you would like to see and, since the collection is so vast, it is wise to concentrate on only one section on each visit. The museum provides 'quiz trails' for teachers to use, but they are ideal for parents and children too (just ask at the information desk). Basically, they are maps with different routes around the museum, focusing on a particular topic, such as the 'Tutankhamun Trail' which, takes you round the Egyptian rooms.

Alternatively, if you want to get a flavour of the range of items displayed here, the highlights of the museum are described below. They are well signposted and many stand on their own podiums away from the other displays. Also, look out for the gallery which opened in 1995 on Hellenistic art.

On the ground floor: the Assyrian lion hunt reliefs dating from the reigns of King Ashurbanipal (668–627 BC) and his grandfather Sennacherib (704–681 BC) at Nineveh; the Indian bronze sculpture of Shiva *c.* AD 950; the Lindisfarne Gospels, English illuminated manuscripts produced at the monastery of Lindisfarne in the seventh century; and two of the four originals of the Magna Carta.

On the upper floor: the Egyptian mummies; the walrus ivory chessmen found on the island of Lewis in 1831; the Lindow Man – the twisted and tortured-

The British Museum

looking remains of a ritually slaughtered ancient Briton preserved in a peat bog for over 2,000 years; the Mildenhall Treasure – a set of Roman silver tableware found in Suffolk in the 1940s; the Portland Vase – a cameo glass production, with the top layer carved to reveal the blue underneath; and the Sutton Hoo treasure – a seventh-century Anglo-Saxon burial ship found in Suffolk in 1939.

Amenities include a shop, café and restaurant.

⊖ Goodge Street, Holborn, Russell Square, Tottenham Court Road

🚌 10, 24, 29, 73, 134

♿

Open: Monday–Saturday, 10.00 a.m.–5.00 p.m; Sunday, 2.30 p.m.–6.00 p.m.;

(clearance of the galleries begins about 10 minutes before closing time)

Free (but donations welcome)

Natural History Museum

Cromwell Road, SW7 (0171 938 9123)

See also page 46

A blend of Victorian curiosities and specimens, giant dinosaurs and modern research, the Natural History Museum offers a fascinating glimpse into the history of nature.

On entering the museum you come face to face with a life-sized plaster-cast skeleton of a dinosaur, the 135-million-year-old *Diplodocus*. The museum is divided into two parts: the Life Galleries and the Earth Galleries. The Life Galleries deal with species that are alive today and include sections on British birds, invertebrates and whales (look up at the huge model of a blue whale above you here), while the Earth Galleries examine species that are now extinct.

The Earth Galleries, Natural History Museum

On the first floor are galleries full of various stuffed animals, while over in the Eastern Gallery is an exhibition on 'Our Place in Evolution' and sections on minerals, rocks, gemstone and meteorites.

The Dinosaur Galleries are among the most spectacular (and spine-tingling) in the museum. Huge, life-sized replicas give a good idea of the scale of natural life in prehistoric times and there is also an unnervingly realistic animated model of three *Deinouchys* dinosaurs dining on a freshly killed *Tenoutosaurus*.

Although this part of the museum might frighten very young children, overall this is very much a place that children enjoy. The 'Dinostore' outside the exhibition is particularly popular, and here you can buy a range of souvenirs all with a dinosaur theme.

Many of the galleries at the Natural History Museum have interactive exhibits and the information about each exhibition is clearly presented. The museum also produces a selection of themed activity sheets for children which they can take round the museum.

Don't forget to visit the Discovery Centre in the basement too. Here, there is plenty for inquisitive hands and eyes to explore, from 'feelie' boxes to put your hands in and see what's inside to microscopes to investigate. This is a busy activity room, full of experiments to carry out and specimens to touch. For example, you can make your own seeds and see how they are carried by the wind and have a look at what can be found on the seashore. There are games too which help children learn about the difference between warm and cold objects. 'Explainers' are on hand to provide more information about individual activities.

Outside is a wildlife garden, specially created to encourage wildflowers, frogs and other garden animals to thrive. Opened in 1994, there are already over 950 trees and 3,800 shrubs. Tours, lasting about 45 minutes, are available twice daily.

The museum organizes a wide range of events for visitors of all ages, including video showings, children's workshops, theatrical events and family lectures.

θ South Kensington

🚌 C1, 9, 14, 52, 74

♿

Open: Monday–Saturday, 10.00 a.m.–5.50 p.m.; Sunday, 11.00 a.m.–5.50 p.m. (closed 23–26 December)

£ (free after 4.30 p.m. on weekdays and after 5.00 p.m. on Saturday and Sunday; under-fives are free always)

Science Museum

Exhibition Road, SW7 (0171 938 8080; 0171 938 8008: recorded information)
See also page 46

A vast display of scientific achievements, the Science Museum successfully combines technology and education to create one of the most enjoyable museums in London. This is somewhere most children will definitely want to come back to again and again. The basement area has been given over to kids and has been an instant success since it opened in September 1995. The first room you arrive at down there is 'The Garden', which is aimed at three- to six-years-olds, a hands-on gallery for fun and learning. Children put on bright-coloured aprons to stop them getting too mucky and then they can get down to some serious fun. The water section – a large tank full of dams, pumps and buttons – teaches children about the properties of water, from building dams to how rain falls.

One corner of 'The Garden' is devoted to understanding building. Hard hats are provided (!) and children can build with giant plastic building blocks or even learn how to tile a roof, with large sponge-shaped tiles. Other activities include playing and learning about reflections and noise.

If it all gets too much (it does get noisy at busy times), younger children (and their parents) can retreat into a large bright pink skip and play with the toys inside.

Further along the basement is the 'Secret Life of the Home' gallery which unfolds the mysteries of domestic gadgets. Next to this is 'Things'. Aimed at older children (seven- to eleven-years-olds), this is a themed interactive gallery that makes children question the purpose of ordinary things. By touching, pushing and squeezing various buttons, they can find out.

Another interactive gallery is the Launch Pad (shown right). Here, you have the chance to try out and participate in all sort of simple scientific experiments, from becoming part of an electric circuit to seeing how sound waves work. This gallery is very popular (it's fascinating seeing how both adults and children become totally absorbed in the gadgets), so you may have to queue to get in at busy times.

Other sections at the Science Museum that appeal to children include the 'Food for Thought' exhibition (first floor). This is an engrossing guide to how science and technology have affected what we eat and how it is prepared. You can also see how much our diet has changed over the twentieth century.

Also, make time to go 'On Air' (third floor). Of interest to older children (twelve years upwards), this exhibition takes you into the world of radio broadcasting. There is a mock-up of a DJ's studio and aspiring DJs can have a go at mixing a record themselves.

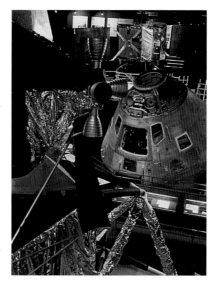

If there is time, there are plenty of other exhibits to see – here are some highlights. On the ground floor are the large and heavy steam boilers, turbines and electric engine, as well as the *Apollo 10* spacecraft and other underwater and space exploration vehicles (right).

The first floor has more machines, showing the development from hand to machine tools, as well as the history of telecommunications, time-measuring and astronomy. The second floor looks at other sciences — chemistry, mathematics, computers and nuclear physics — while one floor up you can learn about magnetism, electricity, acoustics, photography and the history of the cinema.

Medical history can be explored on the fourth floor (with plenty of gory antique medical instruments on view), and on the fifth floor the exhibits show the history of science and the art of medicine around the world.

⊖ South Kensington

🚌 C1, 9, 14, 52, 74

♿

Open: daily, 10.00 a.m.–6.00 p.m.

£ (free after 4.30 p.m.; under-fives are free always)

The Victoria & Albert Museum

South Kensington, SW7 (0171 938 8500)

A jewel in London's cultural heritage, the Victoria & Albert Museum, better known as the V & A, is home to the world's greatest collection of decorative art and design. Its galleries reflect centuries of achievement in such varied fields as ceramics, sculpture, furniture, jewellery, metalwork, textiles and dresses, from Europe, the Far East, South Asia and the Islamic world.

The dress collection is a glittering visual display of social history. Spanning four centuries of fashion, this gallery traces the development of European fashion and style chronologically.

The twentieth-century galleries are great fun too — here you will see the great design classics of this century.

Family programmes take place throughout the year. The museum regularly

Tipu's Tiger, one of the many intriguing artefacts at the V&A

produces a leaflet listing what's on called 'Events at the V&A: A Programme of Drop-In Activities'. Gallery trail notes are also available for some permanent exhibitions – pick them up at the information desk.

⊖ South Kensington

🚌 C1, 14, 74

♿

Open: daily, 10.00 a.m.–5.50 p.m. (Monday, from 12 noon)

£ donation expected

SPECIAL INTEREST MUSEUMS

ENTERTAINMENT

Madame Tussaud's

Marylebone Road, NW1 (0171 935 6861: recorded information)

Without doubt one of the most popular exhibitions in London; the constantly long queues to enter in the summer can be avoided by booking tickets in advance. Madame Tussaud herself was a Frenchwoman born in 1761. Her widowed mother was a housekeeper to a doctor who taught the girl wax modelling skills. Her work at a Paris exhibition led to an invitation to the court of Louis XVI and Marie Antoinette, where she supervised the artistic education of the King's sister for nine years before the Revolution broke out. Her connection with the royal family made her 'guilty by association' and she was imprisoned, sharing a cell with the future Empress Josephine and only narrowly escaping the guillotine. On her release she was compelled to make death masks of executed nobles; some of these masks can still be seen in the museum.

She moved to Britain and for the next thirty-three years she travelled all over the country exhibiting her collection of models. In 1835 she established a permanent base in London, known as 'The Bazaar, Baker Street', visitors being charged sixpence for admission. In 1884 her grandsons moved the exhibition to its present site.

The museum aims to have some topical displays by including authentic waxworks of the latest celebrity, pop star or sportsman (Paul Gascoigne with his wax figure is pictured below). In the Grand Hall you will find historical, political, military and royal figures, while in the refurbished Chamber of Horrors notorious criminals are re-created almost too realistically with spine-chilling sound effects.

If you are also visiting the London Planetarium, the combined admission ticket saves money.

⊖ Baker Street

🚌 2, 13, 18, 82, 113

Limited ♿

Open: October–March, daily, 10.00 a.m.–5.30 p.m.; April–September, 9.00 a.m.–5.30 p.m.

££

Museum of the Moving Image (MOMI)

South Bank, Waterloo, SE1 (0171 401 2636: recorded information)
See also page 44

Become the star of the latest blockbuster movie in an interview with film journalist Barry Norman, fly high over London like Superman or even read the 'News At Ten' during a visit to the Museum of the Moving Image. The museum utilizes many ingenious displays to illustrate the history and magic of cinema and television in a journey through time. From early Chinese shadow theatre, you pass to the birth of television and international cinema up to the latest in television technology. Look out for the actor-guides in costume bringing the exhibits to life and try out for yourself some basic animation techniques.

Nothing has been overlooked at this award-winning museum that is packed with original posters, film and television clips and costumes, notably Marilyn Monroe's 'shimmy dress' from *Some Like It Hot*. Allow an absolute minimum of 2 hours to visit this entertaining and educational museum that appeals to both adults and children. Facilities include a shop and a café.

⊖ / ▣ Waterloo

🚌 26, 68, 168, 171, 188

♿

Open: daily except 24–26 December, 10.00 a.m.–6.00 p.m. (last admission 5.00 p.m.)

£

Puppet Centre

Battersea Arts Centre, Old Town Hall, Lavender Hill, SW11 (0171 228 5335)
Formed in 1974 to promote the arts of puppetry and animation, the Puppet Centre has an excellent collection of puppet figures, rare photographs, slides, posters and memorabilia on display at the Battersea Arts Centre and in the Art of the Puppet touring exhibition. The Puppet Centre can give information about puppet theatre performances in venues across London. Puppet performances are given regularly too (see page 143).

▣ Clapham Junction

🚌 77, 77A

♿

Open: Puppet Centre: Monday–Friday, 2.00 p.m.–6.00 p.m.

Free

Rock Circus

London Pavilion, Piccadilly Circus, W1 (0171 734 8025)
The history of rock 'n' roll through the ages is told through a series of tableaux featuring life-size wax models of all the major stars, from Elvis Presley to Madonna. The highlight of the exhibition is a rock show where the waxwork stars appear to come alive and dance and play along to their greatest hits. See also Pepsi Trocadero, page 35.

⊖ Piccadilly Circus

🚌 3, 14, 19, 22, 38, 53

♿

Open: June–August, daily, 9.00 a.m.–10.00 p.m. (Tuesday, from 12 noon; Friday and

Saturday, to 11.00 p.m.); September–May, daily, 10.00 a.m.–10.00 p.m. (Tuesday, from 12 noon; Friday and Saturday, to 11.00 p.m.)

££

Shakespeare's Globe Exhibition and Guided Tour

New Globe Walk, Bankside, SE1 (0171 928 6406)

Destroyed by fire in 1613 when an ember from a stage cannon used in a performance of *Henry VIII* set light to the thatch, the original Globe Theatre was a famous Elizabethan theatre where many of Shakespeare's plays were performed. The theatre has been rebuilt as an entertainment, education and cultural complex.

The Globe is a celebration of Shakespeare's life and work – a living, working theatre, performing his plays in the open air to audiences seated on wooden benches just as three centuries ago. In their special exhibition you can see craftsmen using seventeenth-century techniques to complete the timber-frame construction of the new Globe Theatre. The exhibition also tells the history of the old theatre and describes the research that has gone into the design for the new one.

⊖/🚇 Cannon Street, London Bridge

🚌 P11, 344

Limited ♿

Open: daily, 10.00 a.m.–5.00 p.m.

£–££ (including guided tour)

The Theatre Museum

Russell Street, Covent Garden, WC2 (0171 836 7891; 0171 836 2330: box office)

Situated in the heart of Theatreland, the Theatre Museum is a celebration of 400 years of Britain's theatrical heritage. Despite its name, the museum actually covers all live performing arts, including circus, magic, opera and ballet.

A costume workshop at the Theatre Museum

The museum's excellent permanent collections form the basis of temporary exhibitions that explore the British stage and its stars. Theatrical history is told using a wealth of costumes, props, drawings, photographs, posters and audio-visual displays. In your journey through the museum look out for the reconstructions of early theatres including the 1614 Globe, and a display illustrating the restoration of the Savoy Theatre to its Art Deco form of 1929.

Included in the price of the entry ticket is the daily tour guide service, costume workshops and make-up demonstrations. Children particularly enjoy these, especially when they see their friends transformed into animals!

It is a good idea to phone in advance to find out about temporary exhibitions, events and talks. The museum also has a souvenir shop and a box office should you wish to step straight out of the museum and into a West End production.

⊖ Covent Garden

🚌 6, 9, 11, 13, 23

♿

Open: Tuesday–Sunday, 11.00 a.m.–7.00 p.m.

£

HERITAGE AND HISTORY

The Bank of England Museum

Bank of England, Bartholomew Lane, EC2
(0171 601 5545)

Housed within the Bank of England (see page 19) at the heart of the City of London, this museum traces the history of the Bank from its foundations by Royal Charter to the high-tech world of modern banking.

There are gold bars dating from ancient times to the modern market bar, coins and a unique collection of banknotes. There are also items you might not expect to find in a bank, such as the pikes and muskets used to defend the Bank and the Roman pottery and mosaics uncovered when the Bank was rebuilt in the 1930s.

The Bank Stock Office, a late eighteenth-century banking hall by the great British architect Sir John Soane, has been reconstructed and inter-active videos give the opportunity to look behind the doors of the nation's central bank. Live information on gilt-edged stock and securities and the foreign currency and money markets is given at the Dealing Desk, similar to those in everyday use at the Bank.

⊖ Bank

🚆 Cannon Street (weekdays only), Fenchurch Street, Liverpool Street

🚌 8, 11, 15, 22B, 26

♿

Open: Monday–Friday, 10.00 a.m.–5.00 p.m.

Free

Cabinet War Rooms

Clive Steps, King Charles Street, SW1 (0171 930 6961)
Enter the Cabinet War Rooms tucked away in a corner of Whitehall at the centre of British government, and you feel as if you have stepped back through history to the dark days of the Second World War. The Cabinet War Rooms were moved here for safety in 1939 and it was here that Winston Churchill worked and lived with his ministers and war workers while planning the British strategy for winning the war against Germany.

In the Cabinet Room the clocks are set at 16.58 and the tables have been prepared as they were for a Cabinet meeting, while in the floor below are the dormitories where the workers slept. Other rooms include the Transatlantic Telephone Room, adapted in 1943, that housed a direct telephone link between Churchill and the American President, Franklin Roosevelt, the Map Room, Room 60A, a typing area which provided a 24-hour service and Room 60 Left, which held BBC Radio transmitting equipment. Churchill broadcast four major speeches from his office-bedroom further along the corridor which were then relayed from Room 60 Left to the outside world.

⊖ Westminster
🚌 3, 11, 24, 77A, 211
Limited ♿

Open: daily, 10.00 a.m.–6.00 p.m. (1 April–30 September, from 9.30 a.m.); last admission 5.15 p.m.)
£

Geffrye Museum
See page 40

Horniman Museum
Forest Hill, SE23 (0181 699 1872)
The museum was set up by Frederick John Horniman MP, a wealthy Victorian businessman who made his money in tea and was a major enthusiast of anthropology. His museum contains displays on the cultures, traditions and changing living conditions of the peoples of the world and origins and customs of different religious beliefs.

Equally interesting are the displays of musical instruments from all parts of the world and from all musical traditions. In the Music Room Gallery you can experience the instruments yourself and the music they create by using the headphones provided. There is also a video that explores the

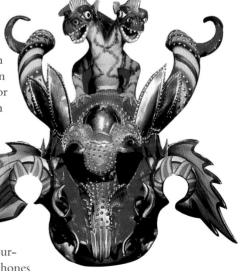
Bolivian devil mask

❖

making, playing and mechanics of the French horn. Handling sessions using instruments are arranged in the central activity area. Performances and demonstrations are also held. The museum holds regular workshops for children and adults. There is a café and souvenir shops.

🖳 Forest Hill

🚌 P4, 122, 176, 185, 194

♿

Open: Monday–Friday, 10.30 a.m.–5.30 p.m.; Sunday, 2.00 p.m.–5.30 p.m.

Free

London Dungeon

28–34 Tooley Street, London Bridge, SE1 (0171 403 0606: recorded information)
Not for the faint-hearted, the London Dungeon cleverly manages to create a gruesome atmosphere where you can frighten yourself out of your wits.

Passing through the cold, damp candlelit 'dungeons', you discover a history of blood-thirsty and barbaric methods of punishment used in Britain over the centuries re-created in tableaux. The story begins with a human sacrifice at Stonehenge by Druids and Boadicea spearing a Roman soldier to death. Punishments were still fairly barbaric in Tudor times and you can see Anne Boleyn, one of Henry VIII's less fortunate wives, being beheaded. Other highlights include the revamped 'Jack the Ripper Experience' with new special effects and the 'Theatre of the Guillotine'. Although this museum is often fascinating, it can be a welcome relief once you reach the end and daylight outside.

The London Dungeon is unsuitable for children under ten.

⊖/🖳 London Bridge

🚌 P11, 35, 40, 47

♿

Open: daily, April–September, 10.00 a.m.–5.30 p.m.; October–May, 10.00 a.m.–4.30 p.m.

££

Museum of Mankind

Ethnography Department of the British Museum,
6 Burlington Gardens, W1 (0171 437 2224;
0171 323 8043: information desk)
The Museum of Mankind is all about the variety of non-western societies and cultures. Its collections includes masks, textiles and costumes from the native peoples of Africa, Australia and the Pacific Islands, North and South America, as well as from contemporary cultures.

⊖ Green Park, Piccadilly Circus

🚌 9, 14, 19, 22, 38

♿

Open: Monday–Saturday, 10.00 a.m.–5.00 p.m.; Sunday, 2.30 p.m.–6.00 p.m.

Free (£ for some exhibitions)

National Postal Museum

King Edward Building, King Edward Street, EC1
(0171 239 5420)

For over 350 years the British Post Office has provided postal services to the public and today the Post Office and Royal Mail are part of our everyday lives. This museum takes you through the history of the postal system, from the Penny Black (*right*) to the latest issues, along with early examples of letter boxes, post horns, medals, stamp boxes and model mail coaches.

⊖ Barbican, St Paul's

🚌 8, 22B, 25, 56

Limited ♿

Open: Monday–Friday, 9.30 a.m.–4.30 p.m. (closed bank holiday Monday)

Free

LONDON

London Canal Museum

12–13 New Wharf Road, King's Cross, N1 (0171 713 0836)

The museum tells the history of the development of London's canals and gives an intriguing insight into the people who strove to make a living from their boats. It is housed in a former warehouse built in the 1850s for Carlo Gatti, a famous ice-cream manufacturer. Blocks of ice were imported from Norway and carried on

People still make a living from the canals today (see pages 117–18)

the Regent's Canal from the dock at Limehouse to Battlebridge Basin. Beneath the warehouse there are two vast ice wells, one of which has been partly excavated and is now on show to the public.

⊖ 🚇 King's Cross

🚌 10, C12, 17, 18, 30, 45, 46, 63, 73

No ♿

Open: Tuesday–Sunday, 10.00 a.m.–4.30 p.m.

£ (free for under-eights)

London Transport Museum

Located in the heart of London's Covent Garden, the London Transport Museum has been specially designed with children and families in mind. Completed redeveloped in 1993, the museum is bright and airy with newly created upper levels offering visitors a unique perspective of the impressive collection of historic buses, trams and trains. Complementing the display of vehicles are galleries housing originals of the famous Underground map and colourful posters from the extensive collection of transport art.

The museum tells the story of transport and travelling Londoners from 1800 to the present day. The hands-on exhibits, working models and touch-screen displays are an easy and exciting way for children to learn about the past while

---

Famous Londoners

Many famous historical figures, including writers, artists, doctors and scientists, have lived in London for at least part of their lives. Some of their homes are now open to the public. They are fascinating places to visit because, as well as being museums of their work, they show how people lived during that period.

Although Charles Dickens lived at 48 Doughty Street, WC1, for only two years, from 1837 to 1839, it was then that he established his reputation as one of Britain's greatest writers. It was the house in which he finished *The Pickwick Papers* and worked on *Oliver Twist*, *Nicholas Nickleby*, *Barnaby Rudge* and *Sketches of Young Gentlemen* and *The Lamplighter*. It is now a museum, library and headquarters of the Dickens Fellowship (0171 405 2127).

⊖ Chancery Lane, Holborn, Russell Square

🚌 19, 38, 45, 55, 68

Limited ♿

Open: Monday–Saturday, 10.00 a.m. –5.00 p.m.

£

having fun at the same time. Children can even sit in the driving seat of a bus or tube train simulator, or listen to the hiss and thump of railway tracks changing and horses clattering through cobbled streets.

The displays are also brought to life every day by actors playing a variety of characters from the past such as a Victorian street sweeper, a 1906 tunnel miner, and a Second World War bus conductress. There are special performances throughout school holidays.

For children wanting to delve further into transport history, the museum has its own Resource Centre where reference books, videos and microfiche records of the archives can be seen without prior appointment. The Resource Centre also contains a database of 5,000 London Transport posters on CD-ROM, which children can look through with the help of a member of staff.

The museum offers a full programme of activities and events from storytelling to children's workshops. An action-packed club for five- to twelve-year-olds, the Wheelie Club, entitles members to free admission to the museum plus a host of special activities.

The shop has a wide range of books, souvenirs and gifts, including reproductions of London Transport's famous posters, while the Transport Café overlooking Covent Garden Piazza is open all day for snacks and drinks.

⊖ Covent Garden

🚌 6, 9, 11, 15, 23

♿

Open: daily, 10.00 a.m.–6.00 p.m. (Friday, from 11.00 a.m.); last admission 5.15 p.m.

£ (under-fives free)

Museum of London

London Wall, EC2 (0171 600 3699; 0171 600 0807: recorded information)
The imaginative displays, some with sound effects, make this museum a great place for even quite young children to learn about the history of London and its people. You can stroll down a replica of a Victorian street with various shops. You can stand in an eighteenth-century prison cell or admire the magnificent stagecoach used by the Lord Mayor of London in 1757. Film shows are also given regularly and a whole range of special events are held here.

There is a shop and in summer you can have a picnic on the lawns outside.

⊖ Bank, Barbican, St Paul's

🚌 8, 22B, 56

♿

Open: Tuesday–Sunday, 10.00 a.m.–5.50 p.m. (Sunday, from 12 noon)

£ (under-fives free)

Ragged School Museum

46–50 Copperfield Road, Bow, E3 (0181 980 6405)

This is the East End's own history museum with a special focus on the work of Dr Barnardo and the development of education in London. It is based in a Victorian warehouse which from 1896 was part of the largest Ragged (free) School in London, known as the Copperfield Road Ragged School. From 1877 to 1908 thousands of poor local children received a free education with free meals in the winter and help towards finding their first job.

As well as displays on Dr Barnardo and the school, there is a re-created Victorian classroom used by school groups for re-enacted Victorian lessons. There is also a lively programme of varied events for children, families and adults, such as treasure hunts and Christmas traditions workshops, while the history club gives regular talks on the East End on the third Wednesday of the month during the winter.

⊖ Mile End

🖳 Limehouse

DLR Limehouse

🚌 D6, D7, 25, 277, 309

No &

Open: Wednesday and Thursday, 10.00 a.m.–5.00 p.m.; first Sunday of each month, 2.00 p.m.–5.00 p.m.

Free, but donations welcome

Sherlock Holmes Museum

221b Baker Street, NW1 (0171 935 8866)

Possibly the most famous address in London, 221b was the home of Sir Arthur Conan Doyle's fictional detective, Sherlock Holmes. Since 1990, this museum has brought to life the house that Holmes shared with his partner Dr Watson. It has been faithfully re-created according to the book and devotees have a chance to see the famous first-floor study where they worked, as well as Mrs Hudson's (the housekeeper) rooms and the bedrooms of Watson and Holmes. Memorabilia from the adventures and a selection of letters written to and from Mr Holmes are also on display, along with a magnificent bronze bust of the detective himself.

⊖ Baker Street

🚌 2, 13, 82, 113, 274

No &

Open: daily, 9.30 a.m.–6.00 p.m. (last admission 5.30 p.m.)

£

Tower Bridge Museum

See page 26

Tower Hill Pageant

Tower Hill, EC3 (0171 709 0081)

This dark-ride experience is a relaxing and enjoyable way to learn about the history of London. The exhibition was made possible through the archaeological finds of the Museum of London during

Tower Hill
by District Line

The Tower of London, HMS Belfast, St Katharine's Dock, River Trips to Greenwich and Westminster ...
and a fabulous view from the top of Tower Bridge
All a few steps from Tower Hill Station

Go Green. Go District.

digs on London building sites. By piecing together their finds as clues they have been able to bring to life the history of London's waterfront is a brand new way.

You sit in a car and are gently transported through time, while a Cockney-accented narrator explains the animated model scenes you pass. Although the story is fairly straightforward, the pace is a bit fast for young children to take it all in – but they can enjoy the spectacular visual effects.

Afterwards, take a look at the exhibition of over 1,000 Roman and medieval finds unearthed by the Museum of London archaeologists.

⊖ Tower Hill

🚇 Fenchurch Street, London Bridge

🚌 15, 42, 78, 100

Limited ♿

Open: daily, 9.30 a.m.–5.30 p.m. (winter, to 4.30 p.m.)

£–££

MILITARY AND MARITIME

Cutty Sark

King William Walk, SE10

(0181 858 3445)

Queen of the tea clippers, this ship was launched in 1869 at Dumbarton in Scotland. From 1870 to 1877 she worked as a tea clipper and it is through this that she became well known, achieving the fastest voyage from China to England in 1871, completed in 107 days with a crew of twenty-eight. In the latter part of the nineteenth century she was employed in the Australian wool trade. Since 1954, she has been in dry dock and is both a wonderful historical relic and a museum with hundreds of nautical artefacts, including brass instruments, paintings and figureheads.

🚇 Greenwich

DLR Island Gardens, then foot tunnel to Greenwich

🚌 177, 180, 188, 199, 286

No ♿

Open: April–September, daily, 10.00 a.m.–6.00 p.m. (Sunday, from 12 noon);
October–March, daily, 10.00 a.m.–5.00 p.m., (Sunday, from 12 noon)

£

HMS *Belfast*

Hay's Galleria, Vine Lane, Tooley Street, SE1 (0171 407 6434)

The *Belfast* (11,500 tons) was a Second World War cruiser that saw service with the Arctic convoys and on D-day. Today, visitors can enjoy exploring the ship from the quarterdeck up to the top of her bridge and all the way down through seven decks to her massive boiler and engine rooms, well below the ship's waterline.

On the way, it is possible to see inside her triple 15-centimetre (6-inch) gun turrets, operate her light anti-aircraft guns, explore the heavily armoured shell room and magazines and experience what life was like for her by crew by visiting the cramped mess decks, officers' cabins, galley and sick bay.

⊖/🚆 London Bridge

🚌 P11, 42, 47, 78

No ♿

Open: March–October, daily, 10.00 a.m.–6.00 p.m.;
November–February, daily, 10.00 a.m.–5.00 p.m.

£

Imperial War Museum

Lambeth Road, SE1 (0171 416 5000; 0171 820 1683: recorded information)

See also page 43

You know you've arrived at the right place when you see the two large naval guns at the entrance of this museum. A history of all the military campaigns fought by Britain and the Commonwealth since the First World War is told here through a series of lively and realistic displays, such as the Trench Experience, showing what it was like to be a soldier on the Western Front during

World War I, with a dug-out and first aid post, and an authentic reconstruction of a London street in 1940, during the Blitz, when London was heavily bombed by the Germans.

In addition there are dozens of tanks, guns and models to fire the imagination. You can also go on a simulated fighter plane ride with Operation Jericho on a secret mission.

⊖ Elephant & Castle, Lambeth North, Waterloo

🚆 Waterloo

🚌 C10, 12, 45, 53, 68

♿ (please phone 0171 416 5320 to give 48 hours' notice if possible)

Open: daily, 10.00 a.m.–6.00 p.m.

£ (free after 4.30 p.m.)

National Maritime Museum and Royal Observatory

Romney Road, Greenwich, SE10 (0181 858 4422)

The area around Greenwich has always had a close link with the sea. At the National Maritime Museum you can find out about Britain's marine history from Captain Cook's exploration of the Pacific to Admiral Nelson's famous battles on the high seas. You can see the guns, maps and navigational instruments they used. Modern-day naval equipment is on display too, in the Seapower Gallery. Here you can see what happens in modern submarines and battleships and, in the interactive section, even try out a missile-control system. Children particularly enjoy the 'All Hands' gallery with such hands-on activities as pulling flags and firing cannons!

The Neptune Hall and the Archaeology Gallery will be closed until at least 1998 for restoration work.

The Royal Observatory was built by Sir Christopher Wren on the orders of Charles II. Since 1884 the world has set its clocks according to the time of day on the Meridian at Greenwich, Longitude 0 degrees. Charles II appointed John Flamsteed as his first Astronomer Royal in 1675 to begin work on how to calculate time at sea – an essential requirement for exploring and mapping the globe. The observatory was completed the following year and subsequently extended. It has been completely renovated and you can now see Sir Christopher Wren's Octagon Room and the apartments of the Astronomers Royal, as well as a space station and a sound-light show in the dome with a 71-centimetre (28-inch) telescope, the largest refracting telescope in Britain. On top of one of the towers is a large red ball mechanism erected in 1833. Every day the ball falls at exactly 1.00 p.m. to enable ships in the river to set their clocks accurately.

Next door in the Meridian Building there is a large digital clock which shows Greenwich Mean Time and outside you can stand astride the Greenwich Meridian which runs through the courtyard. There is a machine nearby where you can buy certificates giving the exact time and date you were there.

🚆 Greenwich

🚌 177, 180, 188, 199, 286

Limited ♿

Open: daily, 10.00 a.m.–5.00 p.m. (last admission 4.30 p.m.)

£

❖

SCIENCE AND TECHNOLOGY

BT Museum

145 Queen Victoria Street, EC4 (0171 248 7444; 0800 289 689: recorded information)
BT's museum describes the history of telecommunications through a series of 'touch and try' displays, videos and exhibits. The displays are constantly changing to adapt to the massive leaps in technology and communication that continue today.

⊖ Blackfriars, Mansion House, St Paul's

🚊 Blackfriars

🚌 11, 15, 26

♿ (advance notice preferred)

Open: Monday–Friday, 10.00 a.m.–5.00 p.m. (closed bank holiday Monday)
Free

London Planetarium

Marylebone Road, NW1 (0171 935 6861: recorded information)
A journey through time and space with regular shows and lectures about the planets and stars in our solar system. There are plenty of special effects, enhanced by the installation of the most advanced star projector in the world – the Digistar Mark II. The shows last 30 minutes and start every 40 minutes. No children under five are admitted. If you are also visiting Madame Tussaud's, the combined admission ticket saves money.

⊖ Baker Street

🚌 2, 18, 27, 30, 82

♿

Open: Monday–Friday, 12.20 p.m.–5.00 p.m. (last show starts then); Saturday and Sunday, 10.20 a.m.–5.00 p.m.
£–££

❖

Royal Observatory

See page 71

Science Museum

See page 56

Wellcome Trust

183 Euston Road, NW1 (0171 611 7211: recorded information; 0171 611 8298: advance bookings for large parties, 'Science for Life')

The Wellcome Trust was set up under the will of Sir Henry Wellcome to support research in medicine and allied subjects. At its headquarters in a refurbished 1930s building and in the new 210 Gallery at 210 Euston Road several exhibitions are open to the public. 'Science for Life' is both an explanation and a celebration of biomedical science. It explores the mysteries of the human body, the nature of scientific discovery and the artistry of the scientist. Aimed at the layperson, the exhibition makes biomedics accessible to the ordinary person, with interactive models so you can see your body through the eyes of a doctor and a walk-through cell magnified a million times.

The Wellcome Institute for the History of Medicine is based primarily on the outstanding collection of the Wellcome Institute Library and presents a lively programme of exhibitions on various aspects of the history of medicine.

⊖ Euston, Euston Square, Warren Street

▣ Euston, King's Cross, St Pancras

🚌 10, 18, 30, 73, 91

Limited ♿

Open: Monday–Friday, 9.45 a.m.–5.00 p.m.; Saturday, 9.30 a.m.–1.00 p.m.; closed bank holiday Monday

Free

SPORT

MCC Museum

Lord's Cricket Ground, St John's Wood, NW8 (0171 266 3825: Tours Department)

See also page 82

Lord's Cricket Ground was established in 1787 by Thomas Lord, a keen cricketer and wealthy property developer. It is the home of the Marylebone Cricket Club, founded in 1787 when cricket was emerging from its medieval village roots into a game popular with the aristocracy. The club's leading position was at once recognized and in 1788 it lay down a code of laws. The MCC has been the guardian of the laws of cricket ever since and today receives suggestions from governing bodies worldwide.

The museum is a treasure house of cricketing history. As befits the gentlemanly atmosphere, visitors are encouraged to dress smartly. The highlight of the tour around Lord's is a visit to the Long Room, the inner sanctum where MCC members can watch matches. This is also an art gallery with portraits of Thomas Lord and C.B. Fry, the English all-rounder who was offered, and refused the crown of Albania, together with paintings of other famous cricketing stars, including Douglas Jardine, Sir Pelham 'Plum' Warner, Sir Donald Bradman and W.G. Grace. You can also see a display of bats used by such great stroke players as Trumper, Compton, Hutton and Hobbs. During the non-cricket season (the winter) the tour includes visiting the home dressing rooms.

No visit to the museum would be complete without seeing the famous Ashes. Whoever wins them every two years, England or Australia, they are kept here permanently, safe in a terracotta urn.

Cricket is not the only sport played at Lord's; there has been a long tradition of real tennis too. Henry VIII's favourite game is still played here today and you can visit the unusual tennis courts.

⊖ St John's Wood
🚌 13, 46, 82, 113
Limited &

Open: guided tours (book in advance) at 12 noon and 2.00 p.m. daily (subject to changes in times); no tours during Test and Cup matches

£

The Museum of Rugby

RFU Ground, Rugby Road, Twickenham, Middlesex (0181 892 2000)
Twickenham, home of England rugby since 1909, welcomes visitors. The Museum of Rugby is designed to appeal to enthusiasts of all ages with interactive displays, rugby memorabilia and a continuous film show. 'The Twickenham Experience Tour' gives visitors a fascinating glimpse behind the scenes with a visit to the England dressing room and the players' tunnel.

🚇 Twickenham
🚌 281
&

Open: Museum: non-match days, Tuesday–Saturday, 10.30 a.m.–5.00 p.m.; Sunday, 2.00 p.m.–5.00 p.m. (last admission 4.30 p.m.); match days, 11.00 a.m.–1 hour prior to kick-off (match ticket holders only). Tour: Tuesday–Saturday, 10.30 a.m., 12 noon, 1.30 p.m., 3.00 p.m.; Sunday, 2.30 p.m.

£

TOYS, DOLLS AND TEDDY BEARS

Bethnal Green Museum of Childhood

Cambridge Heath Road, E2 (0181 980 2415: recorded information)
See also page 40
The Museum of Childhood is part of the Victoria & Albert Museum (see page 58) and houses one of the largest toy collections in the world, with unique exhibits including dolls, doll's houses, teddy bears, trains, games and puppets. The museum also exhibits a range of children's costume and nursery furniture in three displays: Birth and Infancy, The Early Years and Breaking Away.

⊖ Bethnal Green
🚌 D6, 8, 106, 253

Limited ♿

Open: Monday–Thursday and Saturday, 10.00 a.m.–5.50 p.m.; Sunday, 2.30 p.m.–
5.50 p.m.

Free

The London Toy and Model Museum

21–23 Craven Hill, Bayswater, W2 (0171 402 5222: recorded information)
See also page 46

Tucked away in a quiet corner of Bayswater is a museum for children of all ages.
A large Georgian town house has been converted into a rabbit warren of rooms,
full to bursting with all sorts of toys, dolls and games.

The museum has a pleasant, intimate feel and there are plenty of buttons for small
hands to push that activate working models, slot machines and toys. Tracing the
history of toys, displays range from an Ancient Roman Gladiator doll to prototype
toys for the twenty-first century in the 'Whatever Next' gallery.

In the garden there is a miniature electric railway, complete with ride-on trains
for small passengers and a cheery café in the conservatory wing.

⊖ Bayswater, Lancaster Gate, Queensway

🚌 12, 94

Limited ♿

Open: Monday–Saturday, 10.00 a.m.–5.30 p.m. (Sunday and bank holiday Monday, from
11.00 a.m.); last admission 4.30 p.m.

£

Pollock's Toy Museum

1 Scala Street, W1 (0171 636 3452)

Behind Charlotte Street in an area of London known as Fitzrovia is a marvellous
old curiosity shop housing Pollock's Toy Museum. In fact the museum covers two
small houses that have been joined together. Inside, you can wander up and down
winding staircases through tiny rooms packed with goodies. There are displays of
toys dating back for several hundred years, including wax and composition dolls,
folk toys, board games, teddy bears and toy soldiers.

The toy theatres are, however, the main feature of the museum. The museum
is named after one of the leading publishers of juvenile drama, Benjamin Pollock
(1856–1937). A furrier by trade, he took over his father-in-law's publishing business on his death and proceeded to publish large numbers of play reprints, as well
as toy theatres and figures.

⊖ Goodge Street

🚌 10, 24, 29, 73, 134

No ♿

Open: Monday–Saturday (except bank holiday Monday), 10.00 a.m.–5.00 p.m. (last
admission 4.30 p.m.)

£

ART GALLERIES

Dulwich Picture Gallery

College Road, Dulwich, SE21 (0181 693 5254)

See also page 43

Opened in 1817, this was the first purpose-built art gallery in England and is one of the most beautiful. In the heart of Dulwich village, it is an ideal place to visit as part of a trip to this pretty corner of London, particularly for those children who might feel overwhelmed by the size of the major galleries. It has an outstanding collection of paintings by old masters, including Rembrandt, Poussin, Claude, Rubens, Van Dyck, Watteau, Gainsborough, Reynolds, Tiepolo and Canaletto.

🚆 Herne Hill, North Dulwich, West Dulwich

🚌 P4

♿

Open: Tuesday–Saturday, 10.00 a.m.–5.00 p.m. (Saturday, from 11.00 a.m.); Sunday, 2.00 p.m.–5.00 p.m.

£ (free on Friday and for children under sixteen)

The National Gallery

Trafalgar Square, WC2 (0171 839 3321; 0171 777 2885: information)

See also page 38

The National is a hugely popular gallery with over four million visitors each year and now houses over 2,300 pictures. Among the best-known works in the National Gallery are 'The Arnolfini Marriage' by Jan van Eyck, 'The Baptism of Christ' by Piero della Francesca, 'The Virgin and Child with Saint Anne and Saint John the Baptist' by Leonardo da Vinci, 'Bacchus and Ariadne' by Titian, 'Le Chapeau de Paille' by Rubens, 'Hay Wain' by Constable, 'The Water-lily Pond' by Monet and 'Sunflowers' by van Gogh.

Temporary exhibitions are frequently held to complement the permanent collection, usually in the Sainsbury Wing exhibition galleries.

A new innovation is the Micro Gallery, where you can view the collection by working a user-friendly touch-screen computer terminal. This enables you to plan your own tour of whatever is of particular interest, whether this is a specific painting, an artist, a period, subject matter or genre. It is free of charge.

Another excellent way to enjoy looking round the gallery is to use the gallery guide soundtrack (suitable for children over eight), available from the distribution desks at the main entrance and at the Sainsbury Wing entrance. You can select commentaries on pictures of your choice in any order you wish. The commentaries will provide information on the subject matter, history, technique and artists.

Organized tours are available twice daily from Monday to Saturday. There are lectures at 1.00 p.m. (Tuesday–Friday; 12 noon on Saturday) at most times of the year and films about artists or schools of painting at 1.00 p.m. on Monday.

⊖ Charing Cross, Embankment, Leicester Square, Piccadilly Circus

🚆 Charing Cross

🚌 3, 9, 11, 24, 29

♿ Orange Street, Sainsbury Wing

Open: Gallery: Monday–Saturday, 10.00 a.m.–6.00 p.m. (Wednesday, to 8.00 p.m.);
Sunday, 12 noon–6.00 p.m.
Micro Gallery: Monday–Saturday, 10.00 a.m.–5.30 p.m.; Sunday, 12 noon–5.30 p.m.
(closed 1 January, Good Friday, May Day holiday and 24–26 December)
Free

National Portrait Gallery

St. Martin's Place, WC2 (0171 306 0055)
Founded in 1856 to collect pictures of royal and political characters, the National
Portrait Gallery brings history to life through its hundreds of portraits of Britain's
most influential and famous figures.

The exhibits are arranged chronologically and at the top
of the building (Level 5) you will find medieval and Tudor
pictures while the Later Twentieth-Century Galleries
(Level 1) feature contemporary portraits from 1945 to
the present day. The Photography Gallery features both
works from the Gallery's photographic collection and
loan exhibitions from contemporary photographers.

Among the permanent collection of the
Twentieth-Century Gallery you will find a host of
well-known personalities, including such sports
figures as cricketer Ian Botham, while from the
world of pop music there is Paul McCartney and
Elton John. Portraits of Her Majesty the Queen
and members of the present royal family are on
display on the mezzanine landing (Level 2).
⊖ Charing Cross, Embankment, Leicester
Square, Piccadilly Circus
▣ Charing Cross
▤ 9, 11, 23, 24, 29
♿ through Orange Street entrance
Open: Monday–Saturday, 10.00 a.m.–6.00 p.m.; Sunday, 12 noon–6.00 p.m. (closed
1 January, Good Friday, May Day bank holiday and 24–26 December)
Free (£ for some exhibitions)

Making a Scrapbook

Instead of cluttering up their rooms with all the tickets and leaflets children
acquire on various outings, these can be kept in a scrapbook as a colourful
record of the places they have visited. Older children can also write notes
about anything that particularly interested them. A map of London's underground railways could be pasted into the front of the scrapbook and the
stations that have been visited marked with a highlighter. This is a fun way of
learning how the different part of London fit together.

Royal Academy of Arts

Burlington House, Piccadilly, W1 (0171 439 7438)

Set in a magnificent eighteenth-century building, the Royal Academy has played a major role in British artistic life for over 200 years. The most popular exhibition is the Summer Exhibition, held between June and August every year since 1769. Over 1,500 pictures by living artists are displayed for sale and any artist can submit up to three works.

⊖ Green Park, Piccadilly

🚌 9, 14, 19, 22, 38

♿

Open: daily, 10.00 a.m.–6.00 p.m.

£ (free to members)

Tate Gallery

Millbank, SW1 (0171 887 8000; 0171 887 8008: recorded information)

See also page 38

The Tate Gallery has a dual role as the museum of British art and of international twentieth-century art. The main galleries are built around a central hall and are spacious and well-lit. As with many of the world's great art museums, the Tate Gallery has not nearly enough space to show all its collection at once. For this reason, the Tate's displays now change each year, while some also change at intervals throughout the year. This programme is called 'New Displays'. Particular schools of artists are represented in depth at the Tate, such as eighteenth-century landscape painting, the Pre-Raphaelites and the London Avant-Garde, 1910–20.

⊖ Pimlico

🚌 2, C10, 36, 88, 185

♿ via Clore Gallery

Open: Monday–Saturday, 10.00 a.m.–5.50 p.m.; Sunday, 2.00 p.m.–5.50 p.m.

Free (£ for special exhibitions)

Wallace Collection

Hertford House, Manchester Square, W1 (0171 935 0687)
See also page 39

Hertford House was the London home of the Wallace family, wealthy art collectors in the eighteenth and nineteenth centuries. Among the superb works of art on view, there are outstanding collections of French eighteenth-century paintings, furniture and porcelain, together with a number of paintings by old masters. Four galleries are devoted to one of the finest collections of arms and armour in England.

⊖ Bond Street, Marble Arch

🚌 2, 13, 30, 74, 113

♿ (phone 0171 815 1350 for more details)

Open: Monday–Friday, 10.00 a.m.–5.00 p.m.; Sunday, 2.00 p.m.–5.00 p.m. (closed 24–26 December, 1 January)

Free

Cartoon Art

The exhibitions of the best of British and international cartoons, caricatures and comic strips at the National Museum of Cartoon Art, Baird House, 15–17 St Cross Street, EC1 (0171 405 4717), may well appeal to some children more than the works of the old masters. They will quickly spot familiar figures in the comic strips.

⊖ Chancery Lane, Farringdon

🚉 Farringdon

🚌 55, 63

♿

Open: Monday–Friday, 12 noon–6.00 p.m.

Free

SPORT

SPORT FOR KIDS

SPORT can range from simply kicking a ball around a park to riding across the bracken in Richmond Park on a misty autumn morning. A particularly fun sport that can involve all the family is orienteering (see page 88). The major centres for this sport are included here, along with tips and information on access to facilities for all the most popular sports in London.

The sports department of each local council is responsible for organizing sports activities in parks in the borough concerned, so if you want to have a casual game of football or rounders in your park, you will need to phone the department first.

There are facilities for athletics, tennis, football, netball, cricket, rounders and softball in nearly every London park. Most parks organize coaching lessons for tennis too, either individually or in groups. In order to use a court or pitch you will need to book (and pay a small fee) first. In some areas, you can turn up at the park's office and book in person; in others you need to go through the local council. You will find the number in the telephone directory listed under the relevant council.

BADMINTON

See Sports Centres on page 95

BOXING

Young boys are legally allowed to take up boxing from the age of eleven (although it is advisable to start training in the gym from age ten). The best way in is to join your local boxing club; phone the London Amateur Boxing Association (0171 252 7008) for details.

CANOEING

See Watersports Centres pages 99–103

CRICKET

One of the best ways for young people to improve their cricket is to take part in a holiday coaching course. The following are particularly recommended.:

MCC Indoor Cricket School
Lord's Cricket Ground, St John's Wood Road, NW8 (0171 432 1014)
The school offers private and group coaching all year round for children aged

eight years and over. There are also after-school and weekend sessions and holiday courses at Christmas, Easter and in the summer.

⊖ St John's Wood
🚌 13, 46, 82, 113
No ♿
££

Surrey County Cricket Club

The Oval, Kennington, SW8 (0171 582 6660)
The club holds structured eight- or ten-week courses during term-time for children aged eight and over. Holiday courses are held at half-terms and holidays for groups, and children do not need to have any cricketing experience.

⊖ Oval
🚌 36, 185
No ♿
££

CYCLING

Both children and adults face the same perils when out on London's streets on a bicycle. Safety is the number one consideration and it is not really advisable for children under fourteen to cycle alone.

There are still plenty of places to explore by bike, such as the wide open spaces of Richmond Park or Hampstead Heath, but remember that cycling is only allowed on the marked cycle paths and it is illegal to stray off these. For more information on cycle routes across London and cycling proficiency courses, check out *On Your Bike*, a useful handbook produced by the London Cycling Campaign, which can be contacted at 3 Stamford Street, SE1 (0171 928 7220).

FOOTBALL

See also page 186
Football in the Community schemes are held by all London's major clubs. A team of coaches from each club provide training and holiday schools all over London for both boys and girls. Phone for information on current courses as arrangements change regularly.

NORTH

Arsenal Football Club

Arsenal Stadium, Avenell Road, Highbury, N5 (0171 704 4000)
General coaching sessions are held during the school holidays, weekends and after school for boys and girls aged seven to fourteen years. Basic skills are taught in all aspects of football, including playing five-a-side games. Match Day packages are

also available which involve training on a Saturday morning and a ticket to a home match in the afternoon.

⊖ Arsenal

🚌 4, 19, 236

No ♿

££

SOUTH

Crystal Palace Football Club

Selhurst Park, Whitehorse Lane, SE25 (0181 771 5886)

For boys and girls aged under twelve Mini Soccer is an excellent introduction to the sport; courses are held at weekends and during holidays. For children aged nine to thirteen there are Striker Courses, held in the holidays. The coaches are all Football Association-qualified, and the most improved young player at the end of the course wins a trophy.

🚉 Selhurst

🚌 68A, 75, 157

No ♿

££

Millwall Football Club

The Den, Zampa Road, Rotherhithe, SE16 (0171 394 9216: enquiries)

The nearby Lion Centre in Bolina Road, SE16, holds a range of football activities for children in association with Millwall Football Club. Weekly coaching sessions for five- to twelve-year-olds take place and a five-a-side league meets on Monday nights. Various holiday activities are also organized.

🚉 South Bermondsey

🚌 P13 (Monday–Saturday)

No ♿

££

Wimbledon Football Club

Selhurst Park, Whitehorse Lane, Thornton Heath, SE25 (0181 771 2233)

Holiday, half-term and after-school courses for children aged five to sixteen take place all year round. There are also 'ordinary' and 'advanced' six-week summer holiday programmes open to both boys and girls.

🚉 Selhurst, Thornton Heath

🚌 68A, 75, 157

No ♿

££

WEST

Chelsea Football Club

Stamford Bridge, Fulham Road, SW10 (0171 385 0710)

Soccer Schools are held every holiday for boys and girls aged six to fourteen, with

CUP FINAL WEMBLEY SATURDAY APRIL 24ᵀᴴ
FROM ANY **UNDERGROUND** STATION

coaching on dribbling, turning, control, passing, heading and shooting skills –
practice in the morning and a game in the afternoon. There is also a Saturday
morning football club. Children need to have a grounding in basic football skills.

⊖ Fulham Broadway

🚌 14, 211

No 👤

££

Fulham Football Club

Craven Cottage, Stevenage Road, Fulham, SW6 (0171 384 3552)
Both boys and girls can enjoy football here. There are girls' football sessions on
Monday evenings, while for boys there is a Saturday morning class for six- to
fourteen-year-olds at the nearby Eternit Wharf Recreation Centre and football
coaching camps in the holidays. The cost of the course includes a ticket to a home
game, and a certificate and a medal after completing the course.

⊖ Putney Bridge

🚌 74, 220

No 👤

££

Queen's Park Rangers Football Club

South Africa Road, Shepherd's Bush, W12 (0181 743 0262)
As well as Open Days where children can come and meet their QPR heroes,
various coaching sessions are held during the holidays. A special treat is the Match
Day package, which comprises a morning of coaching, lunch and then a ticket to
watch QPR play in the afternoon.

⊖ Shepherd's Bush, White City

🚌 283

No 👤

££

GO-KARTING

Playscape Pro Racing

Battersea Kart Raceway, Hester Road (off Battersea Bridge), SW11 (0171 498 0916)
This is the only go-karting course in London that specializes in training children. Suitable for kids aged eight to sixteen. Safety is the prime consideration of the instructors, who make sure that the children are proficient at controlling the two pedals (the accelerator and the brake) on their kart before they are allowed to run in groups of three around the circuit.

Race overalls, crash helmets and gloves are provided and the course can either be booked for individual children or they can attend the Cadet School (usually held on the first Saturday of each month from 9.30 a.m. to 12.30 p.m.) which is better value.

🚉 Battersea Bridge, Queenstown Road, then 15 minutes' walk
🚌 49, 345

Open: Monday–Friday, 9.30 a.m.–5.30 p.m.
££

GYMNASTICS

See Sports Centres page 95

ICE-SKATING

You can usually hire boots on the door. The ice rinks featured here all take children from three upwards.

Broadgate Arena

Eldon Street, EC2 (0171 505 4068)
The arena is used for concerts and street theatre in summer but becomes the only outdoor rink in London between mid-November and March. The rink is also used (by adults) to play the Canadian game of Broomball.

⊖ Liverpool Street
🚌 22A, 47, 78, 149
♿

Open: mid November–March, Monday–Friday, 12 noon–2.30 p.m., 3.30 p.m.–6.00 p.m., also 7.00 p.m.–10.00 p.m. (Friday); Saturday and Sunday, 11.00 a.m.–1.00 p.m., 2.00 p.m.–4.00 p.m. and 5.00 p.m.–7.00 p.m.
£–££

Queen's Ice Skating Club

Queensway, W2 (0171 229 229 0172)
London's most central ice rink, Queen's is always busy. Some of the more experienced skaters tend to race around the rink, which can be a bit unnerving for the less confident, so avoid the busy evening sessions and try to come earlier in the day. Lessons are available for both children and adults.

⊖ Bayswater

🚌 12, 23, 36, 70, 94

No ♿

Open: Monday–Friday, 10.00 a.m.– 4.30 p.m. and 7.30 p.m.–10.00 p.m. (Friday, to 11 p.m.); Saturday and Sunday, 10.00 a.m.–5.00 p.m., also 7.30 p.m.– 11.00 p.m. (Saturday) and 7.30 p.m.–10.00 p.m. (Sunday)

£

Sobell Ice Rink

Hornsey Road, Holloway, N7
(0171 609 2166)

Part of the Sobell Sports Centre, this rink is usually open only in the evenings but during half-terms and holidays it is also often open during the day (times vary so phone first). Lessons are available and can be arranged with the coach on Tuesday evenings.

⊖ Holloway Road

🚌 19, 106, 210, 236

♿

Open: Wednesday, Friday, Saturday and Sunday, 7.30 p.m.–9.30 p.m. (Friday, to 10.30 p.m.)

£

Streatham Ice Rink

386 Streatham High Road, SW16
(0181 769 7771)

Streatham offers ice skating and ice-hockey lessons to children over eight and tuition for four- to five-year-olds.

Open: Monday–Friday, 10.00 a.m.–4.00 p.m. and 7.30 p.m.–10.00 p.m.; Saturday and Sunday, 10.30 a.m.–5.00 p.m., also 8.00 p.m.–11.00 p.m. (Saturday) and 8.00 p.m.–10.00 p.m. (Sunday)

£

KITE–FLYING

Parliament Hill is one of the most popular sites for kite-flying, but any large open space is suitable. Contact the Kite Store at 69 Neal Street, WC2 (0171 836 1666) for information on local kite-flying competitions and meetings.

Top Tips for Kite-flying

In a steady breeze, unwind about 20 metres (65 feet) of string. In strong winds, unwind less string initially and feed it out once the kite is in the air. To launch the kite, get someone to help you by holding the kite as high in the air as possible. You should be up-wind of the kite (the wind blowing on to your back as you face the kite). Make sure that the string between you and the kite has no snags or knots and is stretched out fully.

When there is little or no wind, pull the controls firmly towards you when your companion releases the kite to help it get airborne. If you are flying a kite with two strings (known as an acrobatic kite), make sure each string is wound out by exactly the same amount – otherwise the kite will dive into the ground as soon as it is launched.

Never fly a kite near overhead electric or telephone cables or a pylon; if the kite hits the cable and the string is damp, you could get a fatal electric shock. Avoid wooded areas; trees create turbulence in the air, cut the wind and always seem to tangle around your kite! Make sure that there are no other people close by when you practise flying or if the wind is strong – a kite can easily fall from the sky or get out of control and hit someone.

MARTIAL ARTS

Classes in judo, karate, and tai kwon do are all available to children in London at a large number of sports centres (see page 95) and are very popular. Although martial arts are not necessarily dangerous sports when taught by well-qualified teachers, children should avoid any martial art move that places constant strain on their still-forming bones, such as 'snap punching' in karate, locks in aikido or locks, strangles and sacrifice throws in judo.

ORIENTEERING

Orienteering is an excellent family activity where competitors navigate their way at their own pace between features marked on a special coloured map. An orienteering course varies in length from about 2 kilometres (1¼ miles) with from six to twenty control points for beginners and children to over 12 kilometres for experienced adult orienteers.

Orienteering takes place on a wide range of outdoor sites and in London these vary from local parks to heaths and woods. Permanent courses include:

Abbey Wood, Lesnes Abbey Woods and Bostall Heath, SE2
Barnes Common, SW13
Crystal Palace Park, SE24
Finsbury Park, N4
Hampstead Heath, NW3
Lee Valley Park, E4
Victoria Park, E9

For up-to-date information about permanent orienteering courses in the Greater London area and available maps, contact The Silva Service, Unit 10, Sky Business Park, Eversley Way, Egham, Surrey TW20 8RF (01784 439193)

PRE-SCHOOL PLAY-GYMS

Children as young as four months old can benefit from classes to improve co-ordination and movement.

Crêchendo

St Luke's Hall, Adrian Mews, Ifield Road, SW10 (0171 259 2727)
See also page 184
One of London's leading pre-school play-gyms, Crêchendo has seventeen centres in London (Battersea, Canonbury, Chelsea, Chiswick, Finchley, Fulham, Hampstead, Kensington, Kingston-upon-Thames, Knightsbridge, Maida Vale, Mortlake, Muswell Hill, Notting Hill, Putney, Richmond and Wimbledon), but all bookings are made on the telephone number given above. Babies can attend classes from four months onwards, beginning with the Babyplay classes, which involve singing and playing with toys, and graduating up to Toddlerplay by ten months, Kidsplay by two and Childsplay by three.

Crêchendo provides plenty of stimulating toys and physical play equipment, such as climbing frames and soft play in structured 45-minute classes, and is a great opportunity for both babies and mothers to socialize. Phone for details of cost of ten-class courses and club membership.

Tumbletots

Blue Bird Park, Bromsgrove Road, Hunnington, Hale's End, West Midlands (0121 585 7003; 0181 464 4433 for classes in Dulwich, Clapham and Battersea; 01342 850001 for classes in Barnes, Fulham and Wimbledon)
These classes are similar to those organized by Crêchendo and use specially designed equipment to help children to explore and develop their physical capabilities. Children are divided into different age groups, with the youngest groups (aged six months to two years) concentrating on simple games, singing songs and exploring equipment such as crawling tunnels. Older children (two to five) have more structured classes with the emphasis on improving balance, agility, climbing and co-ordination.

RIDING

There is a surprisingly large number of British Horse Society-approved riding schools in London and these are listed overleaf. The days and times vary depending on the season and lessons should be booked in advance.

CENTRAL

Hyde Park Riding Stables

63 Bathurst Mews, W2 (0171 723 2813/706 3806)

The fun of riding in Hyde Park makes
the hair-raising trip along Bayswater
Road from the stables beforehand
worthwhile. There are twelve horses
in this school and, as well as riding
in the park, you can have lessons in
the two outdoor manèges.

⊖ Lancaster Gate, Marble Arch

🚌 12, 94

No &

££

Ross Nye's Riding Stables

8 Bathurst Mews, W2 (0171 262 3791)

Basic riding instruction is available here, with sixteen horses to choose from
and the chance to ride in Hyde Park's Rotten Row. There is also a children's
pony club.

⊖ Lancaster Gate, Marble Arch

🚌 12, 94

No &

££

EAST

Aldersbrook Riding School

Empress Avenue, Manor Park, E12 (0181 530 4648)

The school currently has twelve horses, a livery yard and two outdoor manèges.
They organize hacks and offer lessons (including some for disabled people).

⊖ East Ham, then bus

🚉 Manor Park, Woodgrange Park

🚌 101

&

££

Lee Valley Riding Centre

Lea Bridge Road, Leyton, E10 (0181 556 2629)

Classes are available for children and adults on twenty-one horses and ponies.
There is an outdoor floodlit manège and an indoor riding arena, a cross-country
course and paddock classes, as well as limited hacking in the adjacent Lee Valley.

⊖ Leytonstone

🚌 48, 56

No &

££

Mudchute Park and Farm Riding School

Pier Street, Isle of Dogs, E14 (0171 515 0749)

The school is part of Mudchute City Farm and is a particularly good place for children (over seven), including absolute beginners and those with special needs, to learn to ride. Instruction is also given in flat work, show-jumping and cross-country. There are week-long summer courses that include the care of horses. Pony rides for under-sevens are available from 2.00 p.m. to 3.30 p.m.

DLR Mudchute

🚌 D7, D8 (Monday–Saturday, not evenings)

♿

£–££

Woodredon Riding School

Upshire, Nr Waltham Abbey, Essex (01992 714312)

Situated in the heart of Epping Forest, this riding school caters for riders of all ages and experience. Facilities include a large covered school, an outdoor manège and a cross-country course.

⊖ Epping, Loughton

🚌 517 (Monday–Saturday, not early mornings or evenings)

No ♿

££

NORTH

Belmont Riding Centre

The Ridgeway, Mill Hill, NW7 (0181 906 1255)

This riding centre offers private and class lessons, as well as hacks. Facilities include a livery yard, two outdoor manèges and an indoor arena.

🚆 Mill Hill

🚌 240

No ♿

££

Kentish Town City Farm

1 Cressfield Close, off Grafton Road, NW5 (0171 916 5420)

There are about nine horses and ponies. As part of the facilities at Kentish Town City Farm, children can also learn to ride.

⊖/🚆 Kentish Town

🚌 C2, 24, 46, 134, 214

No ♿

££

Kings Oak Equestrian Centre

Theobalds Park Road, Crews Hill, Enfield, Middlesex (0181 363 7868)

A large school, with twenty-two horses; lessons are held in either the outdoor manège or indoor arena. There is also a cross-country course for experienced riders.

🚇 Crews Hill
🚌 W10 (Monday–Saturday, shopping hours only)
No ♿
££

London Equestrian Centre

Lullington Garth, Finchley, N12 (0181 349 1345)

This school has forty horses to suit all shapes, sizes and standards. If you have not ridden here previously you will be assessed before you are put into a class to check your ability. Lessons take place in a large, covered arena and an outdoor manège. Jumping lessons are also available and there are field rides in the summer.

⊖ Mill Hill East
🚌 221
No ♿
££

Suzanne's Riding School

Brookshill Farm, Brookshill Drive, Harrow Weald, Middlesex (0181 954 3618)

This riding school is lucky enough to have 81 hectares (200 acres) of grassland to ride on, including a cross-country and show-jumping course, three outdoor all-weather arenas and one indoor school.

⊖ Stanmore, then bus 340 and short walk
🚌 258 (Monday–Saturday)
No ♿
££

SOUTH

Dulwich Riding School

Dulwich Common, SE21 (0181 693 2944)

There are fifteen horses here and the school provides lessons for children over ten and adults under 70 kilograms (11 stone). All lessons are held either in the outdoor manège or indoor arena – both are floodlit.

🚇 West Dulwich
🚌 P4
No ♿
££

Mottingham Farm Riding Centre

Mottingham Lane, SE9 (0181 857 3003)

The grounds here cover 16 hectares (40 acres) of land with a cross-country course and a stream and all lessons are held outdoors. Lessons are for children over three and adults under 82.5 kilograms (13 stone).

🚇 Mottingham
🚌 160
♿
££

Willow Tree Riding Establishment
Ronver Road, Hither Green, SE12 (0181 857 6438)
There are about forty horses here and lessons are held in either an indoor arena or outdoor manège. The school also caters for riders with special needs.
🚆 Lee, Grove Park
🚌 160, 261
No &
££

Wimbledon Village Stables
24 Wimbledon Village High Street, SW19 (0181 946 8579)
Riding takes place on Wimbledon Common, where there is an outdoor ring. Hacking, jumping and dressage lessons are also available, plus 2-hour rides to Richmond Park.
⊖ Wimbledon
🚌 93
No &
££

RUGBY

London has some lively youth rugby schemes organized by the major clubs. Several clubs have mini rugby sides that meet on Sunday mornings. Most take both girls and boys and all offer a great opportunity to obtain top-class coaching and to get involved in tournaments. Children generally have to pay a joining fee for the season.

Other clubs provide 'academies' for would-be Will Carlings, where the emphasis is on learning skills rather than playing in matches.

Saracens RFC
Bramley Sports Ground, Chase Side, Southgate, N14 (0181 449 3770: head office)
Boys only are allowed to join the Saracens mini rugby teams. The teams (Under-7s to Under-17s) meet on Sunday mornings for training or matches.
⊖ Oakwood
🚌 298, 299, 307
No &
££

Wasps RFC
Repton Avenue, Sudbury, Wembley, Middlesex HA30 (0181 902 4220)
Wasps organize an 'academy' for boys and girls aged twelve to seventeen every Wednesday evening during the rugby season.
⊖ North Wembley, Sudbury Town
🚌 H17, 18
No &
Free

RUGBY AT TWICKENHAM BY TRAM FROM HAMMERSMITH OR SHEPHERDS BUSH

London Irish RFC

The Avenue, Sunbury-on-Thames, Middlesex TW16 (01932 882 964)
The London Irish mini rugby teams meet every Sunday morning during the rugby season (September to the end of April). The teams range from the Under-6s to the Under-19s. Girls can play in the teams up to the Under-12s but, due to lack of facilities, only boys can be admitted to teams in the older age groups.

The club welcomes all children, and activities include training and competing in matches and tournaments.

🚉 Sunbury
🚌 216, 235
♿

London Scottish RFC

Richmond Athletic Ground, Kew Foot Road, Richmond, Surrey, TW9 (0181 332 7112)
Young Scots – the club prefers Scottish children – from the ages of six to twelve can join the mini rugby teams that meet every Sunday morning during the rugby season. Training is given and the teams also play in matches. Boys and girls are welcome.

⊖/🚉 Richmond
🚌 H37, 65
No ♿
££

London Welsh RFC

Old Deer Park, Kew Road, Richmond, Surrey, TW9 (01956 505460)
Welsh and non-Welsh children can join the mini rugby teams, which range from Under-7s to Under-12s. Girls and boys are welcome and the teams meet for training and matches on Sunday mornings. There are regular holiday and half-term courses and the highlight of the season is the annual tour to Wales.

⊖/🚉 Richmond
🚌 65
No ♿

SKIING

London may not have any mountains, but there are artificial ski slopes where you can practise before going on holiday.

Crystal Palace National Sports Centre

Ledrington Road, SE19 (0181 778 0131)
It is necessary to book in advance for both private lessons and courses.

🚉 Crystal Palace
🚌 227
No ♿

Open: daily, 9.00 a.m.–10.00 p.m.
££

Hillingdon Ski Centre,

Park Road, Uxbridge, Middlesex (01895 255183)

Children aged four to sixteen can attend courses on Saturday morning or have private lessons throughout the week.

⊖ Uxbridge, then 15 minutes' walk

🚌 U1, U10 (Monday–Saturday, shopping hours)

No ♿

Open: summer, Monday–Friday, 2.00 p.m.–10.00 p.m., Saturday, 10.00 a.m.–6.00 p.m., Sunday, 10.00 a.m.–10.00 p.m.; winter, Sunday–Friday, usually 10.00 a.m. – 10.00 p.m., Saturday, 10.00 a.m.–6.00 p.m.

££

SPORTS CENTRES

There are almost 200 sports centres in London, so there's no excuse not to go along and find out what's on! Many have swimming pools, and organize lessons for all abilities, from water babies to advanced swimmers. On dry land, you will also find a range of activities, from trampolining to table tennis. During school holidays, many sports centres hold special activities and training courses. The following centres have some of the best facilities for children.

CENTRAL

Queen Mother's Sports Centre

223 Vauxhall Bridge Road, SW1 (0171 630 5522)

Activities: badminton, canoeing, diving, football, gymnastics, martial arts, netball, rounders, short tennis and swimming. There are also various activities for under-fives during holidays.

⊖ Victoria, Pimlico

🚉 Victoria

🚌 2, 24, 36, 185, 211

♿

Open: times vary – phone for details

EAST

King's Hall Leisure Centre

39 Lower Clapton Road, E5 (0181 985 2158)

Activities: badminton, basketball, football, judo, netball and swimming. Holiday activities for eight- to sixteen-year-olds also take place, and there is always a bouncy castle for under-fives to enjoy.

🚉 Clapton

🚌 38, 52

♿

Open: times vary – phone for details

Wanstead Leisure Centre

Redbridge Lane, Wanstead, E11 (0181 989 1172)

Activities: badminton, football, gymnastics, rounders and trampolining. Various activities for under-fives and holiday activities are on offer too.

⊖ Redbridge

🚌 66, 366

♿

Open: 9.00 a.m.–10.30 p.m.

NORTH

Britannia Leisure Centre

40 Hyde Road, Islington, N1 (0171 729 4485)

Activities: badminton, basketball, football, gymnastics (including play-gym for under fives), martial arts, netball, squash, swimming, table tennis, trampolining and volleyball. There are also holiday programmes for five- to fourteen-year-olds.

⊖ Old Street

🚌 38, 56, 73

♿

Open: times vary – phone for details

Copthall Centre

Great North Way, Barnet, NW4 (0181 457 9900)

Activities: martial arts, swimming, football courses and Fit Kids aerobics.

🚆 Mill Hill Broadway

🚌 113

♿

Open: 9.00 a.m.–9.30 p.m. (children must leave pool at 8.00 p.m.)

Sobell Sport Centre

Hornsey Road, Finsbury Park, N7 (0171 609 2166)

Activities: badminton, football, gymnastics and table tennis. Holiday activities are held for children aged eight to fifteen.

⊖ Holloway Road

🚌 19, 106

♿

Open: Monday–Friday, 9.00 a.m.–10.30 p.m., Saturday–Sunday, 9.00 a.m.–9.30 p.m.

SOUTH

Brixton Recreation Centre

Brixton Station Road, SW4 (0171 926 9780)

Activities: badminton, canoeing, gymnastics, martial arts, swimming, tennis and trampolining. Occasional Fit Kids classes are held, and there is a summer programme of activities for children. A soft play area is provided for under-fives.

❖

⊖ Brixton

🚌 35, 95

♿

Open: Monday–Friday, 8.00 a.m.–10.00 p.m, Saturday–Sunday, 9.00 a.m.–8.00 p.m.

Crystal Palace National Sports Centre

Ledrington Road, Norwood, SE19 (0181 778 0131)

Activities: badminton, dancing, diving, gymnastics, martial arts, swimming and trampolining. A summer camp of sports activities is held in the school holidays and there is a mini-gym for under-fives.

🚆 Crystal Palace

🚌 63, 157

♿ by special arrangement

Open: Monday–Friday, 8.00 a.m.–10.00 p.m.,
Saturday, 8.00 a.m.–8.00 p.m., Sunday,
8.00 a.m.– 6.00 p.m.

Roehampton Recreation Centre

Laverstoke Gardens, SW15
(0181 871 7672)

Activities: badminton, football, gymnastics, martial arts, netball, table tennis and trampolining. School holiday programmes and activities for under-fives are also available.

🚆 Barnes

🚌 72, 265

♿

Open: Monday–Friday, 9.00 a.m.–10.30 p.m., Saturday–Sunday, 9.00 a.m.–9.30 p.m.

<u>WEST</u>

Jubilee Sports Centre

Caird Street, Queen's Park, W10 (0181 960 9629)

Activities: badminton, basketball, circuit training, cricket, football, gymnastics, martial arts, swimming, table tennis, tennis and trampolining. School holiday activities and events for under-fives are offered too.

⊖ Queen's Park, Westbourne Park

🚌 18

No ♿

Open: Monday–Friday, 7.00 a.m.–10.00 p.m.,
Saturday–Sunday, 8.00 a.m.–8.00 p.m.

SWIMMING

Overleaf are the best outdoor pools for children. Charges vary from pool to pool, and will be approximately the same as your local, public indoor pool.

CENTRAL

Oasis Sports Centre

32 Endell Street, WC2 (0171 831 1804)

You can swim comfortably all year round in this outdoor, heated pool. It is part of a leisure centre with an indoor pool and cafeteria too.

⊖ Covent Garden, Holborn

🚌 14, 19, 24, 29, 38

No ♿

Open: daily, 7.30 a.m.–8.30 p.m.

Serpentine Lido

Hyde Park, W2 (0171 298 2100)

Located in Hyde Park, this is a unique place to swim and sunbathe. Water in the Lido is chlorinated for safe swimming and life-guards are always on duty. There are facilities to help disabled people and poolside activities, including table tennis.

⊖ Hyde Park Corner, Knightsbridge, Lancaster Gate, Marble Arch

🚌 9, 10, 16, 36, 52

No ♿

Open: May–September, daily, 8.00 a.m.–dusk

SOUTH

Tooting Bec Lido

Tooting Bec Lido Road, SW16 (0181 871 7198)

The second largest pool in Europe, Tooting Bec Lido is 91 metres (100 yards) long! Refreshments are available all through the summer.

⊖ Tooting Bec

🚌 249

No ♿

WEST

Hampton Pool

High Street, Hampton, Middlesex (0181 979 9933)

This is a 36-metre (118-foot) heated pool, with refreshment facilities available at peak times. Some fun activities are arranged for younger children in the summer holidays. Keen swimmers can improve their speed and strokes by joining the group called 'Speedo' which meets regularly.

🚉 Hampton

🚌 R68

No ♿

Open: Easter–New Year's Day, daily, times vary – phone for details

Pools on the Park

Old Deer Park, Richmond, Surrey
(0181 940 0561)
The heated outdoor pool is part of Richmond's sports centre, which also has an indoor pool and a gym and holds exercise classes. Refreshments are available from a café inside the building.

⊖/🚈 Richmond
🚌 65
♿

Open: Outdoor pool: usually Easter–end September, daily, 7.00 a.m.–9.30 p.m. (times vary depending on the weather)

WATERSPORTS CENTRES

The following centres offer a variety of watersports. Opening hours vary depending on the time of year and the weather, so it is best to phone first.

CENTRAL

Westminster Boating Base

Dinorvic Wharf, 136 Grosvenor Road, SW1 (0171 821 7389)
Royal Yachting Association and British Canoe Union courses are held here for children over ten and adults up to twenty-three. Activities include canoeing, power-boating and sailing.

⊖ Pimlico
🚌 24
No ♿
££

EAST

Docklands Sailing Centre

Kingsbridge, Millwall Dock, E14 (0171 537 2626)
Open all year; on Saturdays there are special events and courses, while on Sundays anyone can come and join in. Courses on offer include power-boating and instructor courses, shore-based courses, yacht, coastal and ocean master courses, as well as training in skippering, electronic navigation and diesel maintenance.

School holiday activities include a Youth Afloat programme run in conjunction with other centres. Activities include dragon-boating, canoeing, sailing and rowing, as well as bungee-jumping, angling and sub-aqua activities.

DLR Crossharbour, Mudchute
🚌 D7, D8 (Monday–Saturday, not evenings)
♿
££

Laburnum Boat Club

Laburnum Street, Kingsland Road, E2 (0171 729 2915)
Trips are available for parties of twelve people in the club's three narrow boats: *Lady Mildmay, Mildmay II* and *Opportunity*. While on board, you can learn how to work locks and to steer the boat. Instruction on canoeing is also available.
⊖ Shoreditch
🚆 Dalston Junction
🚌 26, 43, 67, 243, 505
♿
£–££

Leaside Young Mariners Youth Club

Spring Lane, Upper Clapton, E5 (0181 806 1717)
Based alongside the River Lea, this club has been running for over thirty years and offers courses on canoeing and mountain biking up to the standards of their governing bodies. It also provides leisure activities to local schools and youth groups, as well as school holiday, weekend and evening activities.
🚆 Clapton, then bus, Stamford Hill, South Tottenham
🚌 253
No ♿
££

Lee Valley Watersports Centre

Greaves Pumping Centre, North Circular Road, Chingford, E4 (0181 531 1129)
Open all year, this centre caters for all ages from eight years upwards and some activity is suitable for disabled people too. Sailing courses are offered at weekends, as well as basic instruction in windsurfing. Instruction in power-boating up to and including the advanced level is also available. The centre also provides the Royal Yachting Association Young Sailors scheme and racing courses. Activities include sailing, windsurfing, waterskiing and canoeing.
⊖ Walthamstow Central, then bus
🚆 Highams Park, Walthamstow Central, then bus
🚌 34
♿
££

Shadwell Basin Outdoor Activity Centre

Shadwell Pierhead, Glamis Road, E1 (0171 481 4210)
Open all year round, this centre offers Royal Yachting Association and British Canoe Union courses to adults and children. Occasional trips away are organized too. Activities include canoeing, dragon-boating, windsurfing, sailing, sub-aqua activities and fishing.
⊖/**DLR** Shadwell
🚌 100
♿
££

Stubbers Adventure Centre

Ockenden Road, Upminster, Essex (01708 224753)

Used primarily by local schools and youth organizations; advance bookings can be made for other groups to participate in summer holiday courses to suit all ages. Activities include canoeing, sailing and windsurfing, as well as archery and a specialized outdoor climbing wall.

⊖/🚇 Upminster
🚌 370
♿
££

Surrey Docks Watersports Centre

Rope Street, off Plough Way, Rotherhithe, SE16 (0171 237 5555)

This centre caters for all ages and abilities, including people with special needs. During the school holidays children can either enjoy the activities for fun, or train to gain British Canoe Union- and Royal Yachting Association-approved certificates. Parents can join in too, and on Sunday you can go along to brush up on your skills in special one-off training sessions. Activities include canoeing, raft-racing, sailing, windsurfing and power-boating.

⊖ Surrey Quays
🚌 199
♿
££

NORTH

Hillingdon Outdoor Activities Centre

Dews Lane, off Harvil Road, Harefield, Middlesex (01895 824171)

Activities and courses are provided for children during school holidays. All courses are Royal Yachting Association, National Schools Sailing Association or British Canoe Union approved. Activities include sailing, canoeing, windsurfing and raft-building.

⊖ Uxbridge, then bus
🚌 U9 (Monday–Saturday, not late evenings)
♿
££

Islington Boat Club

16–34 Graham Street, N1 (0171 253 0778)

Catering for young people between nine and eighteen, this club offers a wide choice of activities, including regular trips away (as far as Europe) and courses to help improve proficiency. Activities include canoeing, sailing and boating.

⊖ Angel
🚌 43, 214
♿
££

The Pirate Club

Oval Road, Camden, NW1 (0171 267 6605)

Situated on the Regent's Canal, the club is open all the year round to young people between the ages of ten and eighteen. The emphasis is on boating, members learning how to handle rowing-boats, skiffs and coracles safely whatever the weather conditions.

⊖ Camden Town

🚌 C2, 24, 29, 134, 274

No ♿

££

Welsh Harp Youth Sailing Base

Cool Oak Lane, West Hendon, NW9 (0181 202 6672)

Part of Barnet Council's Youth Service programme, the Welsh Harp Youth Sailing Base is open for children and adults between nine and twenty-five. Proficiency courses are held and young people work towards British Canoe Union and Royal Yachting Association certificates. Trips away are occasionally organized too. Activities include sailing, canoeing and windsurfing.

🚆 Hendon

🚌 32

♿

££

SOUTH

Danson Park Lake

Danson Road, Bexley, Kent (0181 303 7777)

The centre here is particularly geared towards providing activities for children during the school holidays. These activities include fishing, regattas, water polo and occasional 'whizz trips', when they are taken on a rescue boat to a nearby island, where they are given a talk about the wildlife there. Activities include windsurfing, canoeing, rowing and sailing.

🚆 Bexleyheath

🚌 494 (Monday–Saturday, not early mornings or evenings)

♿

££

Wimbledon Park Outdoor Education and Leisure Facility

Home Park Road, SW19 (0181 947 4894)

Courses recognized by the Royal Yachting Association are offered here for both children over eight and adults. Other watersports include canoeing and wind-surfing. There are also floodlit tennis courts and all-weather facilities for athletics.

⊖/🚆 Wimbledon Park

🚌 156

♿

££

Albany Park Sailing Centre

Albany Park Road, Kingston-upon-Thames, Surrey (0181 549 3066)

This centre is open to any one over the age of eight but it is essential to book in advance on a course – phone for details. Adult courses tend to be held on Tuesday and Thursday evenings, and other weekday nights are set aside for a local youth club. People with special needs are welcome too. Activities include canoeing and sailing.

🚇 Kingston

🚌 65

♿

££

Ravens Ait

Portsmouth Road, Surbiton, Surrey (0181 390 3554)

Used by schools during the week, the club is open to the public on Sundays for sailing. During the school holidays there is a weekly 'Pirate Club' – book in advance to ensure a place. Activities include sailing, canoeing and kayaking.

🚇 Surbiton

🚌 218

No ♿

££

Rickmansworth Windsurfing and Canoe Centre

The Aquadrome, Frogmoor Lane, off Harefield Road, Rickmansworth, Herts (01923 771120)

Catering for youth groups and school children in particular, this centre offers a wealth of activities and courses, including taster sessions, a river tour and fun races. If you want to take it more seriously, you can train for Royal Yachting Association and British Canoe Union certificates. Activities include windsurfing and canoeing.

⊖ Rickmansworth

🚌 R1 (Monday–Saturday, not evenings)

♿

££

Thames Young Mariners

Ham Fields, Riverside Drive, Nr Richmond, Surrey (0181 940 5550)

The centre caters for beginners to advanced-level students and runs Royal Yachting Association and British Canoe Union courses all year round. Trips away are organized too. Multi-activity courses are available during the school holidays. These include canoeing, sailing, windsurfing, kayaking, power-boating, climbing, orienteering and mountain-biking. Specialized instructors for disabled children.

⊖/🚇 Richmond

🚌 K6 (Monday–Saturday, shopping hours), 371

♿

££

OUTDOOR
ACTIVITIES

CHAPTER FIVE

EXPLORING LONDON'S OUTDOORS

FROM the world-famous London Zoo in Regent's Park to city farms and nature reserves, the capital offers an abundant choice of places to visit. Although it may seem a little cruel to keep animals locked up, zoos play a very important role in breeding endangered species, thus helping to maintain the natural balance of the animal world on the planet. London's many city farms are great fun to visit – be prepared to get your hands dirty as staff often allow visitors to muck in with chores around the farm. There are even waymarked 'country' walks, away from the traffic, on the outskirts of the city.

London Zoo

Regent's Park, NW1 (0171 722 3333)

London Zoo is one of the oldest and best-known zoological gardens in the world. It was founded in 1829 to increase our knowledge of animal life and, more than 150 years later, it is still making exciting new discoveries about the world around us.

There are over 12,000 animals in the zoo and there is always something special to watch or participate in, including pelican feeding, spider encounters, shows and rides.

One of the great features is the Touch Paddock, where you can walk up to and touch, see and smell(!) animals including goats, ducks, hens and sheep. If a child wants to know what wool feels like before it is knitted to make a sweater, this is the perfect place to stroke a sheep and find out! The Touch Paddock has farmyard animals from the UK, but to see domesticated animals from around the world, visit the rest of the Children's Zoo. It's fascinating to see the 'farmyard animals' of some other countries, which include camels and even llamas.

If you have a pet, or are thinking of getting a rabbit or cat, visit the Pet Care Centre (in the corner of the farmyard). Not only do they have all the most popular pets, but the staff will show children the equipment needed and how to look after their pets properly.

In the main part of the zoo there are thousands of rare and interesting animals from around the world. There is lots of information on such animals as mammals and insects. Some of the highlights include the Elephant House, where three Asian elephants live side by side with two rare Black Rhinos. A visit to the Penguin Pool is a must too. It is full of all sorts of breeds of penguins that play on the extraordinary ramps and slides. It is not only the penguins that are on display, since the pool itself has been recently restored and is an architectural masterpiece designed by Lubetkin.

One of the main activities of London Zoo is to work for the conservation of species. It is fascinating to see the animals that it is helping to save. The zoo does a lot to protect animals that are being hunted or captured to be sold as rare pets. Even some of the creepiest-looking animals, such as the red-kneed bird-eating spider, are in danger. This huge, hairy, but beautiful spider is under threat from eager collectors who want to keep it as a pet rather than leave it in the wild to survive.

Facilities include a shop, restaurant and café.

⊖ Camden Town, then bus

🚌 274

♿

Open: daily, 10 a.m.–5.30 p.m. (last admission 4.30 p.m.)

££

Battersea Park Children's Zoo

Battersea Park, SW11 (0181 871 7540)

A lively zoo with plenty of opportunity for children to get involved with the animals – there is a special 'animal contact' area where you can mix with goats and pigs. The meerkats are always entertaining and there is also a reptile house, stables, various exotic birds, as well as wallabies and emus from Australia.

⊖ Sloane Square, then bus

🚉 Battersea Park

🚌 44, 137 (Monday–Saturday, not evenings), 137A (Monday–Friday, peak times and Sunday), 344

♿

Open: May–September, daily, 10.00 a.m.–5.00 p.m. (4.30 p.m. last admission); October–April, weekends only

£

CITY FARMS

City farms have sprung up all over London in the past few years, many in some of the most deprived areas of the East End, where they have become a popular feature of the local communities. Although every farm has a similar selection of

animals – chickens, goats, geese, rabbits and guinea pigs seem the most popular – they each have their own unique atmosphere and charm. The most noticeable common feature is the enthusiasm of the staff for their particular farm, which passes down to the volunteers.

College Farm

45 Fitzalan Road, Finchley, N3 (0181 349 0690)
Originally set up as 'Showplace of the Dairy Industry' in 1883, this 4-hectare (10-acre) farm was the first working farm in Britain to become a tourist attraction. It is now a conservation area – the farm buildings are Grade II listed – with cows, pigs, shire horses, ponies, donkeys, rabbits, sheep, chicken and Highland cattle.

Facilities include a picture gallery, visitor centre and a shop selling animal feed, pet food and saddlery. The tea room is open at weekends and on the first Sunday of every month there is a Country Fête from 2.00 p.m. to 6.00 p.m.

⊖/🖳 Finchley Central, then bus
🚌 82, 143, 260, 326
♿

Open: daily, summer, 10.00 a.m–6.00 p.m, winter, 10.00 a.m–5.00 p.m.
£

Corams Fields

93 Guildford Street, WC1 (0171 837 6138)
Right in the heart of Bloomsbury is an unusual 2.8-hectare (7-acre) park which adults are allowed to visit only if they are accompanied by a child. Part of the site is devoted to a mini city farm and there is also an aviary. The playground areas include a big paddling pool and there are good sports facilities with floodlighting for older children. The children's nursery is very popular.

⊖ Russell Square
🚌 45, 68, 91, 168, 188
♿

Open: March–October, daily, 9.00 a.m–6.00 p.m.; November–February, daily, 9.00 a.m–dusk.
Free

Deen City Farm

39 Windsor Avenue, Merton Abbey, SW19 (0181 543 5300)
The farm has been open since 1980 and is home to sheep, pigs, goats, rabbits, chickens, guinea fowl, horses and ponies. Spinning, weaving and dyeing classes for adults are also held here – phone for details.

Facilities include a farm shop selling eggs, a registered riding school and a visitor centre.

🖳 Mitcham
🚌 200
♿

Open: Tuesday–Sunday, 9.00 a.m.–dusk
Free

Freightliners Farm

Paradise Park, Sheringham Road, Holloway, N7 (0171 609 0467)
A 1-hectare (2½-acre) working farm with cows, sheep, pigs, goats, geese, chickens
and ducks. There is also a classroom for educational projects (phone for details)
and a budding wildlife garden. Volunteers are welcome.

Facilities include a visitor centre and farm shop selling a variety of produce,
including manure!

⊖ Highbury & Islington, Holloway Road
🚌 43, 271
♿

Open: Tuesday–Sunday, 9.00 a.m–1.00 p.m. and 2.00 p.m.–5.00 p.m.
Free, but donations welcome

Hackney City Farm

1a Goldsmiths Row, E2 (0171 729 6381)
A wonderfully converted brewery complete
with a cobbled yard forms the centrepiece of
this farm in the heart of the East End. Meet
cattle, sheep, chickens, turkeys, pigs, ducks,
rabbits and guinea pigs. There is also a small
orchard, an ecological area and wildlife pond,
a vegetable plot and a herb garden. You can
learn all sorts of skills here too, from animal
feeding and gardening to spinning, weaving
and pottery. There are special activities for
children and the handicapped.

Facilities include a café and visitor
centre.

⊖ Bethnal Green
🚆 Cambridge Heath
🚌 26, 48, 55
♿

Open: Tuesday–Sunday, 10.00 a.m.–4.30 p.m.
Free

Kentish Town City Farm

Cressfield Close, off Grafton Road, NW5 (0171 916 5420)
See also page 91
One of London's oldest city farms, established in 1973, this farm has a friendly,
easy-going atmosphere, making it particularly popular with children. As well as all
the usual farm animals, such as cows, pigs and goats, there is a children's garden, a
pensioners' garden and a developing nature area.

⊖ Gospel Oak, Kentish Town
🚌 C11, 26, 46
♿

Open: Tuesday–Sunday, 9.00 a.m.–6.00 p.m.
Free

Mudchute Park and Farm

Pier Street, Isle of Dogs, E14 (0171 515 5901)
See also page 91
Mudchute Park and Farm was created in the last century when silt from the construction of surrounding docks was dumped and a natural wilderness grew up. For decades it remained an East End secret, until 1977, when the Mudchute Association was formed to preserve and develop the area and farm animals were introduced.

It is now a working farm and animal attractions include horses and ponies, sheep, cattle, goats, pigs, chickens, ducks, geese, rabbits, guinea pigs and even a llama and a ferret.

Facilities include a café and a shop.
DLR Mudchute
🚌 D7, D8 (Monday–Saturday)
Limited ♿
Open: daily, 9.00 a.m.–5.00 p.m.
Free

Newham City Farm

King George Avenue, Custom House, E16 (0171 476 1170)
An immaculate farm just a stone's throw from London's City Airport, the main feature here is the 'farm club', through which volunteers can muck in with all sorts of farm work. There is also a fascinating collection of llamas, as well as sheep, cows, geese, ducks, hamsters, ferrets and guinea pigs.
🚉 Silvertown and London City Airport
DLR Royal Albert
🚌 276, 300
♿
Open: Tuesday–Sunday, 10.00 a.m.–5.00 p.m.
Free

Spitalfields Farm Association

Weaver Street, E1 (0171 247 8762)
The warm welcome and lively atmosphere on this farm, built on railway wasteland in the heart of the East End, makes Spitalfields one of the most appealing farms in London. The staff encourage a hands-on approach for visitors, with the emphasis on training and education. There is a horticultural training scheme for school leavers, adult education classes, horse and cart tours and other activities for young and old. Animals include goats, hens, horses, rabbits, ducks and guinea pigs.
⊖ Shoreditch, Whitechapel
🚌 8
♿
Open: Tuesday–Sunday, 10.00 a.m.–5.00 p.m.
Free

Stepney Stepping Stones Farm

Corner of Stepney Way and Stepney High Street, E1 (0171 790 8204)

Animals here include donkeys, ferrets, chipmunks, ducks, hens, sheep, rabbits, guinea pigs, quails, cows, goats and pigs. There is also a fully equipped classroom with a qualified teacher and a wildlife area.

Facilities include a combined café and shop.

⊖ Whitechapel
DLR Limehouse
🚌 309
♿

Open: Tuesday–Sunday, also bank holiday Monday, 9.00 a.m.–6.00 p.m.
Free

Thameside City Farm

40 Thames Road, Barking, Essex (0181 594 8449)

Lying in the middle of a barren industrial estate is a small haven for farm animals, wildlife and children! Much hard work has gone into developing this site, which is now home for several ponies, donkeys, goats, as well as geese and chickens. There is also open pasture which has been given over to wildlife and a black-smith's forge.

Facilities include a café and picnic areas.

🚊 Barking
🚌 369, 387
♿

Open: daily, 10.00 a.m.–5.00 p.m.
Free

Vauxhall City Farm

24 St Oswald's Place (but entrance in Tyers Street), Lambeth, SE11 (0171 582 4204)

An excellently equipped city farm with plenty of facilities, overlooked, bizarrely, by the new Government Intelligence office in Vauxhall. There are dozens of animals, from pigs, piglets, rabbits and sheep to ducks, geese and hens. Children can also ride on the two ponies and the donkey.

Facilities include a shop, a visitor centre and a spinning and weaving club.

⊖ Kennington
🚌 322
♿

Open: Tuesday–Thursday, Saturday and Sunday, 10.30 a.m–5.00 p.m
Free

WILD LONDON

The following wildlife areas and nature reserves are all reasonably accessible for wheelchairs, although it is not always possible to take them off pathways and on to rougher land.

NATURE RESERVES

Bentley Priory Open Space and Stanmore Common

Old Lodge Way, Stanmore, Middlesex

The 66 hectares (163 acres) of meadows and ancient woodland include a 3.6-hectare (9-acre) nature reserve. Wander past the grazing cattle to see an area unusually rich in wildlife; at least eighty species of birds have been seen here and 200 flowering plants. There are two reasonably short, waymarked walks from Stanmore Common and Old Redding car parks.

Θ Canons Park, Stanmore

🚌 142, 340

♿

Open: daily

Free

Boston Manor Nature Trail

Boston Manor Road, Brentford, Middlesex

A trail runs from the lake at Boston Manor Park through the wood, across the River Brent, under the M4 and on to Clitheroes Island. Then it passes the lock gates and on to the Grand Union Canal towpath. A leaflet is available.

Θ Boston Manor

🚌 E8

♿

Open: daily

Free

SUMMER OUTINGS
BY PRIVATE BUS

Camley Street Natural Park

Camley Street, NW1 (0171 833 2311)

An innovative and internationally acclaimed natural park created on the banks of the Regent's Canal, Camley Street has been painstakingly created to provide a natural environment for birds, bees, butterflies, frogs and toads, as well as for a rich variety of plant life.

There is also a visitor centre/classroom well stocked with information leaflets.

🚆/Θ King's Cross

🚌 C12 (Monday–Saturday), 46, 214

♿

Open: Monday–Thursday, 9.00 a.m.–5.00 p.m. (November–March, to 4.00 p.m.); Saturday–Sunday, April–October, 11.00 a.m.–5.00 p.m., November–March, 10.00 a.m.–4.00 p.m.

Free

Crane Park Island

via Crane Park, Ellerman Avenue, Twickenham, Middlesex

Surrounded by the beautiful River Crane, this man-made island is a mosaic of woodland, scrub and meadow. Its unusual history began when the island was created in 1776 to provide water for a gunpowder mill. When the mill closed in 1926, the island developed into a woodland and all that is left of its industrial past is the imposing Shot Tower nearby. In the centre is the millpond, which supports amphibians, grasses, willow, nettles and butterflies.

🚆 Whitton

🚌 H22, 111

♿

Open: daily

Free

Lavender Pond Nature Park

off Rotherhithe Street, SE16 (0171 232 0498)

This nature park was created in 1981 in the northern part of the former Surrey Commercial Docks. Close to the park is the Pumphouse, an old pumping station which now houses an Environmental Studies Centre and the Rotherhithe Heritage Museum.

The water in Lavender Pond is fresh and clear and supports a great variety of animals and plants, including dragonflies and water skaters. Water birds, such as moorhen, mallards and even swans, visit the pond as its edges provide a protected nesting place.

⊖ Rotherhithe

🚌 P11, 225 (Monday–Saturday)

♿

Open: most weekdays and some weekends; please phone for details

Free

London Butterfly House at Syon Park

London Road, Brentford, Middlesex (0181 560 7272)

Tropical greenhouse gardens and ponds with hundreds of free-flying butterflies from all over the world. Among the most interesting are the giant blue morpho, owl butterfly, postman, flambeau and tree nymph. Displays of insects under glass include locusts, scorpions, spiders, stick insects and leaf-cutting ants.

🚆 Kew Bridge

🚌 116, 117, 237, 267

♿

Open: daily, summer, 10.00 a.m.–5.00 p.m.; winter, 10 a.m.–3.30 p.m. (closed 25–26 December)

£

Natural History Wildlife Garden

Natural History Museum, Cromwell Road, South Kensington, SW7 (0171 938 8000)
See also pages 46 and 55
Situated in the south-western corner of the museum's grounds, the Wildlife Garden, covering roughly 0.5 hectare (1 acre) in area, represents a range of British plant and wildlife habitat, including a chalk meadow, bluebell woods, three ponds and a waterfall. Its primary purpose is as an educational tool for children, as well as offering excellent opportunities for scientific research, especially in the field of urban ecology.

⊖ South Kensington
🚌 74
♿

Open: daily, 10.00 a.m.–5.30 p.m.
Free

Stave Hill Ecological Park

Timber Pond Road, Rotherhithe, SE16 (0171 237 9175: answerphone)
Stave Hill has become a haven for butterflies, with over twenty species visiting this rich mosaic of wild flowers, woodland and shrub. In recognition of this diversity, the park has been designated Britain's first urban butterfly sanctuary, forming part of a wider campaign by Butterfly Conservation – a national group striving to redress the decline in Britain's butterfly population. New projects include an orchard, fungi garden, school nature plots and a hop garden. For more information contact the site manager.

⊖ Rotherhithe
🚌 P11
♿

Open: daily
Free

BIRD-WATCHING

Reservoirs are excellent places to find more unusual birds and are important wildlife areas. You will need a permit to visit them; details are given below, along with London's main bird-watching sites.

Barn Elms Reservoir

Merthyr Terrace, off Castelnau, Barnes, SW13
(01734 593363: Recreation Manager)
This is an excellent bird-watching location, within easy reach of central London. Over 200 different types of birds have been recorded, including thirty-one species of wildfowl, thirty-three species of wader and two species of gulls and terns. Shovellers and tufted ducks also come here in winter.

Tips for identifying birds

Bird-watching is great fun, but remember that it does takes practice to be able to identify what you see. If you are a beginner, one of the best ways to start is to take a notebook and pencil with you when you go for a walk.

When you see a bird you do not recognize, first compare it with birds you already know. Ask yourself such questions as, is it smaller than a pigeon? or, is it the same colour as a sparrow? Make notes about shape, the type of legs, bill and wings and if there are any unusual markings or features.

Another point to note is where you saw it, as a bird's habitat will also help to identify it. Check all your information with a bird guide and hopefully you will be able to identify it.

If children are interested in bird-watching and bird conservation, they can join the young ornithologists' section of the Royal Society for the Protection of Birds, which holds regular events and activities. The nearest branch to contact is the south-east office at 8 Church Street, Shoreham-by-Sea, West Sussex, BN43 5DQ.

Many gulls roost here during the winter too, while spring and autumn bring migrants, such as waders, terns, gulls, wagtails, warblers and swifts.

⊖ Hammersmith, then bus

🚌 33, 72

&

Open: daily, 7.30 a.m.– sunset

££ (for permits)

Kempton Park West

Sunbury Way, Hanworth, Middlesex
(01734 593363: Recreation Manager)
Since this reservoir was drained, the resulting marshy grassland, reedbeds and willow scrub have provided temporary habitats for warblers and wildfowl such as teals.

🚆 Sunbury

🚌 216, 290

&

Open: Monday–Wednesday, 7.30 a.m.– 4.30 p.m., Thursday–Friday, 7.30 a.m.–3.30 p.m.

££ (for permits)

King George V Reservoirs

Lee Valley Road, Chingford, Essex E4 (0181 808 1527: Gatehouse)
A Site of Special Scientific Interest, this is an area of national importance for waterfowl, with large numbers of moulting tufted duck in late summer and goosanders, golden-eyes and black-necked grebes in the winter. Terns, little gulls,

pipits, wagtails and buntings, plus a wide selection of waders, can also be seen.

🚉 Brimsdown, Ponders End

🚌 191

♿

Open: daily, 7.30 a.m.–1 hour after sunset (closed 25–26 December)

££ (for permits)

Maple Lodge

Denham Way, Rickmansworth, Herts WD3
(01923 230277: Membership applications)
The diversity of habitats at this site, run by the Maple
Lodge Conservation Society for its members, includes
woodland, meadow, farmlands, ponds and a lake,
encouraging animal and bird life of many kinds.
Wildfowl, waders, owls and woodpeckers may all be
seen and there are several bird hides overlooking the
lake and feeding areas. The area is also rich in moths,
butterflies, small mammals and plant life.

🚉 Maple Cross

♿

Open: members only; please phone for more information.
Visits by schools and youth groups can be arranged

Walthamstow Reservoirs

Ferry Lane, Tottenham, N17 (0181 808 1527: information)
A Site of Special Scientific Interest; the main features are the large heronries on
the reservoir's small islands and a cormorant roost. Rarities include sabine gulls,
little egrets and green–winged teals.

🚉 Blackhorse Road, Tottenham Hale

🚌 W4, 123

♿

Open: daily, 7.00 a.m–1 hour after sunset (closed 25–26 December)

££ (for permits)

Walton Reservoirs

Hurst Road, Walton-on-Thames, Surrey, and Hersham Road, Sunbury, Upper Haliford,
Surrey (01734 593363: Recreation Manager)
These reservoirs are noted for the wintering flocks of diving ducks, such as the
golden-eye, as well as for shovellers, gadwalls, teals and wigeons. Late summer
brings the moulting tufted duck, while other birds include the red-breasted
merganser. A key can be obtained from the gatehouse at Walton.

🚉 Sunbury, Walton-on-Thames

🚌 218 (to Hersham Road)

♿

Open: Monday–Thursday, 7.00 a.m.–5.00 p.m., Friday 7.00 a.m.–1.30 p.m.

££ (for permits)

WALKS AND CANAL TRIPS

The Thames Path is the newest National Trail in England and runs from the Thames Barrier in Greenwich to the river's source at Kemble in Gloucestershire. Managed by the Countryside Commission, this unique path is the only long-distance route in Britain to follow a river throughout its length and to pass through major towns and cities.

It is now possible to walk 64 kilometres (40 miles) along the towpaths of the Grand Union Canal and Regent's Canal from Limehouse in Docklands to Rickmansworth. Some 10 kilometres (6 miles) represent the Brentford arm of the Grand Union, while the remainder forms a continuous route. The route takes in the new Mile End Park, Victoria Park, Regent's Park and Primrose Hill, Horsenden Hill and 11 kilometres (7 miles) of the Colne Valley Park. A booklet on exploring London's canals is available from the London Canals Project Officer, British Waterways, Canal Office, Delamare Terrace, London W2 6ND (0171 286 6101). The less energetic may prefer to explore the canals in one of the narrow boats.

CANAL TRIPS

Canal Cruises

250 Camden High Street, NW1 (0171 485 4433/6210)

Jenny Wren makes a round trip from Camden Town past London Zoo and Regent's Park, to Little Venice and back, with an interesting commentary on the canal's history. *My Fair Lady* was built as a cruising restaurant in the manner of the traditional canal narrow boats. The trips run to Little Venice and back, and include a three-course meal en route.

Θ Camden Town

🚌 24, 134, 168, 214

♿ (phone in advance)

Trip times: vary; please phone in advance

The Floating Boater

1 Bishops Bridge Road, London, W2 (0171 724 8740)

Two charter boats – *Lapwing* and *Prince Regent* – run from Little Venice to Regent's Park, catering for groups and parties. Both boats can be hired out at lunchtime or evening for up to 4 hours. *Lapwing* holds up to to fifty people and offers buffet/cold food only. *Prince Regent* holds just under a hundred people and offers a more extensive, hot menu.

Θ Edgware Road, Paddington (*Lapwing*); Warwick Avenue (*Prince Regent*)

🚌 12, 23, 27, 36, 70

♿ (phone in advance)

Trip times: Lapwing, March–September; *Prince Regent,* March–December

£–££

Jason's Trip

60 Blomfield Road, Little Venice, W9 (0171 286 3428)

Since 1951, Jason's Trip has been taking visitors along the canal from Little Venice to Camden Lock market in traditional narrow boats. At their base in Little Venice, you can wait for your boat in a delightful courtyard where there is a small coffee shop. In the summer there are also inclusive teatime cruises with afternoon tea, and evening cruises with traditional fish and chips. Trips to the London Canal Museum are available as well.

⊖ Warwick Avenue

🚌 6, 46

♿ (phone in advance)

Trip times: April–October, 10.30 a.m., 12.30 p.m., 2.30 p.m.; and June–August (weekends and bank holiday only), also 4.30 p.m.

£–££

London Waterbus Company

Camden Lock, Camden Town, NW1 (0171 482 2550)

Using three traditional, painted narrow boats, a scheduled service runs between Little Venice and Camden Lock. There are also special day trips across north and east London, including King's Cross, Islington and Victoria Park and then on either to the River Lea or to Limehouse Basin.

⊖ Camden Town, Warwick Avenue

🚌 12, 23, 27, 36, 70

Trip times: boats depart every hour in summer and every 1½ hours in winter (weekends only)

£–£

GUIDED WALKS

There are several companies which provide a wide range of walking tours through London. The length of the walks varies from a couple of hours to a whole day and they are geared to suit all ages. They are a great way to meet people and to learn more about parts of London that you are usually too busy to notice. To go on a walk, meet your guide and fellow walkers just outside the designated meeting place at the stated time. Most walks last about 2 hours and end near Underground stations. It is often not necessary to book and walks take place rain or shine, so you may need an umbrella.

London Silver Jubilee Walkway

This circular 19-kilometre (12-mile) walk was created for the Queen's Silver Jubilee in 1977. It starts at Leicester Square, passes through Westminster and over to Lambeth Bridge, then along the south bank to Tower Bridge and back through the City, Fleet Street, Holborn and Covent Garden. The route is marked by 400 large discs set in the pavement and is easy to follow.

❖

Original Ghost Walks

(0171 256 8973)

The London Ghost Walk is a night of magic, music and mystery suitable for children aged eight years and over. To get you into the atmosphere, the guide is dressed up as a Victorian undertaker and takes you through the alleys and back lanes of the City into pubs and churches where you will hear tales of legendary ghosts. Among the most spooky is the legend of a little girl who accidentally hanged herself when she tripped over a piece of rope on the site of the Baynard Castle pub in Lower Thames Street in the 1890s at 5.30 a.m.. Her spirit apparently triggers off an alarm clock every day without fail at this exact time!

Θ Blackfriars

🚌 45, 63, 76, 172, 609

♿

Meet every evening from April to October (November–March, Saturday and Sunday only) at 8.00 p.m. at the exit of Blackfriars tube

£

Original London Walks

(0171 624 3978)

London's longest established walking tour agency boasts an impressive list of tour guides and an interesting and wide selection of walks. These include 'The London of Shakespeare and Dickens', 'Jack the Ripper Haunts', 'The Old Jewish Quarter', 'Legal London', 'The Beatles Magical Mystery Tour' and 'Historic Greenwich'. Phone for details of current programme. If you want to go on several walks, ask for a Discount Walkabout Ticket, which is excellent value for money.

£ (no charge for children under fifteen if accompanied by an adult)

'COUNTRY' WALKS

These walks are not suitable for wheelchair users as they cross rough terrain, but the more urban walks should pose no problems.

Croham Hurst Woodland Ramble

Two circular walks through attractive woods are described in a brochure available from the Croydon Information Centre. These guide you through the woods and even explore a Bronze-age burial barrow and hut circle. For more information, write to Croydon Information Centre, Katherine Street, Croydon, Surrey, or phone the Parks Department on 0181 686 4433.

🚉 East Croydon

🚌 60, 109, 166, 197, 264

Green Chain Walk

The Green Chain comprises a string of nearly 300 of the finest open spaces in south-east London, including parks, gardens, woods, commons, playing fields, golf courses and farmland. Its aim is to preserve and enhance these open spaces, prevent further building from taking place and improve sport and recreation facilities here. The Green Chain Walk is a 63-kilometre (39-mile) waymarked walk linking all the open spaces from Thamesmead to Beckenham, through the boroughs of Bexley, Greenwich, Lewisham and Bromley.

The walks are broken up into manageable chunks of about 6.5 kilometres (4 miles) each and pass some wonderful views and numerous historic sites, such as Eltham Palace, which has an impressive Great Hall and moat bridge, built in 1475, and the ruined monastery in Lesnes Abbey Woods. Other noteworthy sites include Charlton Park and House, one of the best examples of Jacobean architecture in the country, and Severndroog Castle – a magnificent folly erected in 1784. Four leaflets cover the whole of the route.

1. Thamesmead to Oxleas Wood (or Erith)

This walk covers just under 10 kilometres (6 miles) from the riverside on the south bank of the Thames at Thamesmead through Lesnes Woods to Oxleas Wood, Shooters Hill, part of the old Roman Road to London. A 4-kilometre (2½-mile) branch from the riverside at Erith connecting with the main route at Lesnes Abbey is also described.

2. Thames Barrier to Oxleas Woods (or Bostall Woods)

This is a 7-kilometre (4¼-mile) walk from the Thames Barrier on the south side of the River Thames, via Charlton Park to Oxleas Wood, Shooters Hill. Another walk of just under 6.5 kilometres (4 miles) from Charlton Park via Plumstead Common to Bostall Woods, connecting with the Thamesmead route, is also described. This link forms a 9.65-kilometre (6-mile) circular walk.

3. Oxleas Wood to Mottingham

It is 6.5 kilometres (4 miles) from start to finish on this walk, although there are alternative longer and shorter routes: a western route through Eltham Park South and almost a mile longer eastern route through Avery Hill Park and New Eltham. A short link between the two routes connecting Conduit Head with Avery Hill Park allows for two circular walks of 5 and 6 kilometres (3 and 3¾ miles) to be made.

4. Mottingham to Crystal Palace Park (or Chislehurst)

This is a much longer walk, covering 13 kilometres (8 miles). Alternative routes are provided between Mottingham and Beckenham Place Park, with a northern walk through Grove Park and Downham and a southern section, 1 kilometre (½ mile) longer, between Elmstead Woods and Sundridge Park. A link between the two routes connecting Grove Park Hospital through Chinbrook Meadows to Elmstead Woods allows for two circular walks of 5 and 10 kilometres (3 and 6½ miles) to be made. A 3-kilometre (1¾-mile) branch from Elmstead Woods to Chislehurst Common is also described.

Leaflets and more detailed information on all these walks are available from the Director of Leisure Services, Bromley Civic Centre, Stockwell Close, Bromley

BR1 3RU (0181 464 3333). In addition to the walks information, a general leaflet containing a fold-out map of the Green Chain, with a summary of planning policies, is also available from the same address.

🚉 Abbey Wood, Beckenham Hill, Belvedere, Crystal Palace, Eltham, Falconwood, Grove Park, Mottingham, New Eltham, Welling, Woolwich Dockyard

🚌 177, 180, 229, 272, 469

Horsenden Hill Circular Walk

This is a 2-hour, 4.4-kilometre (2¾ mile) leisurely walk across open space, woods and fields. The grassy hill gives spectacular views across as far as Hampstead to the east and Box Hill to the south on a clear day. Other highlights you will see are the remains of an Iron Age hill fort and archeological remains.

A leaflet for the walk is available from Brent River Park Environmental Centre, Brent Lodge Park, Church Road, W7.

⊖/🚉 Perivale

🚌 297

Parkland Walk

Walk along the railway line that used to connect Finsbury Park station and Alexandra Palace, running through Queen's and Highgate Woods. It is also an important local nature reserve, where 32 per cent of Britain's breeding butterfly species can be found and fifty-three species of birds, as well as 233 different kinds of flowering plants.

Start: Oxford Road, N4 or Finsbury Park

⊖/🚉 Finsbury Park

🚌 W3, 4, 19, 29, 253

Finish: Muswell Hill, at entrance to Alexandra Palace and Park

⊖ Highgate

🚉 Alexandra Park

🚌 W3, 43, 134

Charity walks

Charity walks are often advertised in the local national press and on posters. They are becoming a popular way to raise money and, as they are usually a relaxed affair with the emphasis on fun, the whole family can join in.

The Strollerthon, a fun 16-kilometre (10-mile) carnival-style stroll around London, is one of the biggest. About 15,000 people a year take part to help raise money for children's charities, so it is worthwhile participating for at least part of the distance.

For more details, write to Cadbury's Strollerthon, 70 St Marychurch Street, London SE16 4HZ.

PLAYGROUNDS AND PARKS

Parks are Londoners' gardens, where children have the space to run around freely under adult supervision. The best parks for children to explore and those which have the best activities are included below. The parks and open spaces featured are open daily from dawn to dusk, unless otherwise stated.

Although most parks have some play facilities, for a really good time you can't beat an adventure playground. These have been specially built for young adventurers and will typically feature towers, slides, swings and climbing equipment. All adventure playgrounds are legally obliged to be covered with special soft rubber flooring. There are numerous adventure playgrounds in London (phone the parks department of your local council for details). The following are the biggest and the best.

Battersea Park Adventure Playground

Battersea Park, SW11 (0181 871 7539)
The playground caters for children aged five to sixteen. Under-fives may attend if accompanied at all times by a responsible adult, but they may have to leave the playground at peak times if older children's play is too boisterous.

There is also an indoor space that offers a wide variety of workshops, including photography, ceramics, video and drama as well as simple board games and a space to meet.

⊖ Sloane Square, then bus
▣ Battersea, Queenstown Road
🚌 137 (Monday–Saturday, not evenings), 137A (Monday–Friday, peak hours and Sundays)
Open: term-time, Tuesday–Friday, 3.30 p.m.–6.00 p.m., school holidays, Tuesday–Friday, 11.00 a.m.–6.00 p.m., Saturday and Sunday, 11.00 a.m.–6.00 p.m.
Free

Holland Park Adventure Playground

Holland Park, W11 (0171 603 6956)
Newcomers (aged five to fifteen) can attend a special session held on the first Saturday of each month (10.30 a.m.–11.30 a.m.) to help them find their way around this adventure playground. A good range of colourful equipment includes rope bridges, towers and slides. There is also an area for under-eights which is equally well served, with the equipment on a smaller scale.

⊖ High Street Kensington, Holland Park.

🚌 9, 10, 27, 28, 94

Open: main playground: daily, 10.00 a.m.–6.00 p.m. (closed for lunch, term-time, Monday–Friday, 1.05 p.m.–2.05 p.m.); under-eights area: open daily, 12.30 p.m.–4.00 p.m. (April–September, extended hours)

Free

Outdoor Handicapped Adventure Playgrounds

Head office: Pryor's Bank, Bishop's Park, Fulham, SW6
(0171 731 1435; 0171 384 2596: minicom)

There are several excellent adventure playgrounds in London designed specifically for disabled children, which are run by the Handicapped Adventure Playgrounds Association in Fulham. During term-time most of the children who use the playgrounds come in groups from special schools. On Saturday and school holidays children are referred to HAPA by parents, social workers and other play providers. In the holidays between twenty and sixty children are registered every day at each playground. Most of these children will stay for the whole day. If you are interested in finding out more about using a playground (opening times will vary), the individual telephone numbers are given below.

Charlie Chaplin Playground

Bolton Crescent, Kennington Park, Kennington, SE5 (0171 735 1819)

It is a real urban site, although some of the visitors include local foxes who play in the hidden areas at the end of the playground.

⊖ Oval
🚌 36, 185
♿
Free

Chelsea Playground

Royal Hospital Grounds, Royal Hospital Road, Chelsea, SW3 (0171 730 4093)

There is a small outdoor play area with both metal and timber-built play equipment and an indoor section where arts and crafts activities take place. Open only on Saturday.

⊖ Sloane Square
🚌 11, 211
♿
Free

HAPA Playspace

c/o Acklam Adventure Centre, 6 Acklam Road, W10 (0181 968 6330)

This is the most recently opened HAPA playground, forming part of the Acklam Adventure Centre.

⊖ Ladbroke Grove
🚌 23, 70
♿
Free

Hayward Playground

Market Road, Islington, N7 (0171 607 0033)

A large outdoor area in this urban site has fixed wooden structures, musical instruments and a pond.

⊖ Islington

🚌 10, C12, 17, 91, 259

♿

Free

Lady Allen Playground

Chivalry Road, Wandsworth Common, SW11 (0171 228 0278)

The playground is situated in a large area of open space on Wandsworth Common. The big, flat-roofed play-building houses a soft-play area and a large kitchen, as well as a small stage for drama activity. Outdoors there are towers and slides as well as a number of fixed musical instruments.

🚉 Clapham Junction, Wandsworth Common

🚌 35, 37, 49, 77

♿

Free

Palace Playground

Bishop's Avenue, Fulham, SW6 (0171 731 2753)

Features of this playground include a large ramp and walkway that lead to a tower and slide.

⊖ Putney Bridge

🚌 74, 226

♿

Free

Camp Beaumont

203–205 Old Marylebone Road, NW1 (0171 724 2233)

One of the longest-established activity holiday organizers, Camp Beaumont offers both day and residential camps. The day camps offer all the thrill of a week's summer camp but on a non-residential basis. They are held at six sites in and near London.

Children are divided into various age groups (three–five, five–twelve and twelve–sixteen) and on arrival are launched into a range of activities, such as archery, arts and crafts, video film-making, circus skills, roller disco and face-painting. There's even time for a mini-Olympics.

Multibase

Swan Island, 1 Strawberry Vale, Twickenham TW1 4RP (0181 744 2083)

Multi-activity day camps provide a range of activities for children aged three to twelve during the Easter and summer school holidays. The camps are held in Roehampton, SW15, and in Ewell, Surrey.

Activities range from archery and other sports and games, to drama, arts and crafts. There are also theme mornings and a Rumpus Room for younger children.

Holiday fun

Holidays can seem to go on forever when you're young. Luckily, London children need never get bored, as there is an enormous range of outdoor activities at hand to enjoy (see Chapters 5 and 6). Day activity camps are very popular and offer an exhaustive selection of things to do. Some schools run camps (phone your local council to find out which ones near you do) and there are also several companies that offer regular camps in various parts of London. Alternatively, most London boroughs organize good-value outdoor activities during the summer holidays. It is best to phone the Parks and Leisure Department of your local council at the beginning of the holidays for details as many activities are organized only a short time in advance.

X.U.K. Activity Holidays

Experience UK Ltd, Poolside Manor, Lyndhurst Gardens, Finchley, N3
(0181 349 1945)

Founder members of the British Activity Holiday Association, X.U.K. organize day camps for children aged three to seventeen years during the Easter and summer holidays in north London. Children are divided into different age groups. Activities range from magic and puppet shows, nature walks and sing-songs for the youngest children to life-saving classes, tennis coaching and judo for older children to enjoy.

ROYAL PARKS

Greenwich Park

Greenwich, SE10
See also page 71

This park was originally created by Henry VI in 1433 as a deer park and for over 250 years had close links with royalty. Canary Wharf in Docklands now dominates the wonderful view across the Thames from the top of the park. About thirty fallow and roe deer are kept in the enclosure here and have been a feature of the park since the sixteenth century.

🚇 Greenwich, Maze Hill
DLR Island Gardens (then by foot tunnel)
🚌 53
〰 from Westminster Pier
♿
Free

Hampton Court Palace Gardens

East Molesey, Surrey (0181 781 9500)

See also page 12

The gardens' most popular features are the famous maze, which is great fun to get lost in, and the Great Vine, which is over 400 years old. It was planted in the 1690s and is now the only remaining part of the wilderness areas of the garden. Nearby are the tiltyards, which were built by Henry VIII for jousting tournaments and now house two restaurants.

🚉 Hampton Wick

〰 from Richmond or Kingston

🚌 111, 216, 411, 461

♿

Open: summer, 9.30 a.m.–6.00 p.m.; winter, 9.30 a.m.–4.30 p.m.

✪ in Bushy Park, no cycling at all in Hampton Court Palace Gardens

Free

Hyde Park

W1

Lying in the heart of the city, this is probably the best-known park in London. The park has also traditionally been a hive of activity. The first football games, known as 'hurling matches', were played here in the 1700s and it was here too that Joseph Paxton built Crystal Palace for the Great Exhibition of 1851. The park is often used for rallies, open-air concerts, fun runs and fireworks displays.

If you are in need of refreshment, there are several kiosks dotted about the park, as well as the Dell Restaurant, which is situated at the Hyde Park Corner end of the Serpentine (open daily, 9.00 a.m.–6.00 p.m. during the height of the season and 9.00 a.m.–5.30 p.m. for the rest of the year).

The Serpentine, Hyde Park

Sports facilities abound here. There are four hard tennis courts which can be booked up to two full days in advance, in person only, for 1-hour sessions (open daily, 8.00 a.m.–1 hour before sunset). The Serpentine Lido is a centre of activity too. Swimming is possible from May to the end of September. Rowing-boats, paddle-boats and canoes can be hired from the boathouse situated on the north side of the Serpentine from March to October. Table tennis is played on the south bank near the Lido. Hyde Park is the only open place in central London where horse riding by members of the public is allowed. For more information on riding schools, see page 90.

⊖ Hyde Park Corner, Knightsbridge, Lancaster Gate, Marble Arch

🚌 9, 12, 16, 36, 73

♿

☼ north towards Paddington and south towards Chelsea between Speakers' Corner and Hyde Park Corner (cycling is not permitted on any other path or bridle ways).

Free

Kensington Gardens

W8

Adjoining Hyde Park, but with a totally different atmosphere, are Kensington Gardens. They are wonderful for children to explore. To the north is the Dogs' Cemetery, founded by HRH the Duke of Cambridge in 1880 for one of his wife's pets. There is also a children's playground nearby and the stump of an oak tree, known as Elfin Oak, full of carved wooden gnomes, fairies and little animals. The oak was first placed here in 1930 and was restored by the comedian Spike Milligan. In the centre of the park is the Round Pond, ideal for model sailing boats, and George Frederick Watt's statue of Physical Energy, a rider on a horse. To the west is the statue of Peter Pan with his fairy entourage (right), not forgetting the more sophisticated sculpture, The Arch, by Henry Moore over the Serpentine.

⊖ High Street Kensington, Knightsbridge, Lancaster Gate, Queensway

🚌 9, 10, 12, 52, 94

♿

☼ on cycle routes which run north–south, and on the road running east – west in front of the Albert Memorial

Free

Regent's Park,

NW1

Parts of this park, such as Queen Mary's Garden, with its extensive collection of roses, are formal, but there are also open spaces to explore and lakes to boat in. The lakes provides homes for many breeds of waterfowl and the Park acts a care and breeding centre for these birds. There are three play grounds for children to enjoy. These can be found near Gloucester Gate, Hanover Gate and St Andrew's Gate.

London Zoo is one of the main attractions of Regent's Park (see page 106). In summer, there is an open-air theatre in the centre of the park and the repertoire always includes a play for children (see page 142). Ball games are permitted and there are several tennis courts.

⊖ Baker Street, Camden Town, Great Portland Street, Regent's Park

🚊 Primrose Hill

🚌 C2, 13, 18, 24, 27, 31

♿ allowed only on the Inner and Outer Circles

♿

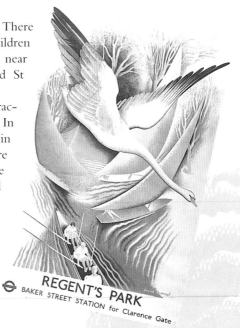

REGENT'S PARK
BAKER STREET STATION for Clarence Gate

Richmond Park

Richmond, Surrey

Both Charles I and Charles II used it as a hunting area – red and fallow deer have always roamed here. Today, two herds of the Queen's deer – 250 red and 350 dappled fallow deer – are allowed to wander free and it is still a treasonous crime to kill one, accidentally or otherwise, so drive carefully!

The park is known today for its wildlife, which includes badgers, its majestic oak trees and the rhododendrons of the Isabella Plantation. There are also marvellous views from the top of the Henry VII mound (said to have been raised to allow the king to survey the field) which extend from Windsor Castle to the dome of St Paul's. As well as being a great place for walking or picnics, there is a wealth of activities to try, from riding and fishing (permit needed) to flying model aeroplanes and playing golf. There is a perimeter road and roads across the park. If you have arrived at Richmond station, use the entrance on Richmond Hill so you can enjoy the spectacular views of Petersham meadow.

Among the houses in the park are Thatched House Lodge, the home of Princess Alexandra; White Lodge, built by George II in 1727 as a hunting lodge and since 1955 the junior section of the Royal Ballet School; and Pembroke Lodge, now a café (see also page 157), standing in 5.2 hectares (13 acres) of its own semi-formal gardens which are worth a wander round. It is open daily during park opening times.

⊖/🚊 Richmond

🚌 65, 371

Limited ♿

Free

St James's Park

SW1

This park has long been associated with unusual and exotic birds. Birdcage Walk is so called after the aviaries built by Charles II. Today the aviaries have gone, but there are an enormous number of birds here still, some tame enough to eat out of your hand. The most famous are the pelicans, who live in a sanctuary by the lake – try to arrive in time to watch them having tea at 3.00 p.m. There are also dozens of friendly, and greedy, ducks, geese, sparrows and pigeons here.

⊖ St James's Park, Westminster

🚌 3, 11, 12, 24, 211

♿

Free

PUBLIC PARKS AND OPEN SPACES

EAST

Epping Forest

Epping Forest Field Centre, High Beech Road, Loughton, Essex

Only a short distance from central London, Epping Forest is an extensive area of ancient woodland. It has a long history and many centuries ago was part of a the huge Forest of Essex which stretched from the River Lea to the sea.

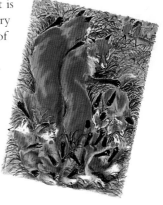

Not all the area is wooded; there are also acres of grass-land, heathland, ponds and even bogs. It is a wonderful place just to wander or to observe the varied plant and animal life. There is a centre which gives information on the forest and organizes courses and guided walks and a woodland path for wheelchairs.

The 24-kilometre (15-mile) Epping Forest Centenary Walk was devised in 1978 to celebrate the centenary of the forest, which was saved from extinction a hundred years earlier by the City of London. Starting at Manor Park Station, the walk crosses Wanstead Flats, Bush Wood, Leyton Flats, Gilbert's Slade, Walthamstow Forest, Higham's Park and along the banks of the River Ching to the Epping Forest Museum and Queen Elizabeth's Hunting Lodge on Ranger's Road. The path then continues past Connaught Water to the Epping Forest Field Centre by the King's Oak pub at High Beech. The end of the route takes you through Little and Great Monk Wood, Ambresbury Banks, and Bell Common to Epping Town.

If the thought of trying to do all the walk at one time sounds a little daunting, do not panic! There are good transport facilities along the way for anyone wanting to break the walk into smaller sections. A detailed leaflet about the walk is available from the Information Officer, Epping Forest Field Centre, High Beech Road, Loughton, Essex IG10 4BL (0181 508 7714).

❖

In addition to the woods and grassland, there are many interesting places to visit. There are two listed buildings in the Forest – Queen Elizabeth's Hunting Lodge at Chingford and the Temple in Wanstead Park. It is also possible to carry out some real countryside activities here – there are bridleways, fishing areas and a model aircraft flying site. Camping is available at High Beech Road, Loughton (phone 0181 508 3749/1000).

Epping Forest is so vast that is its best to travel by car – there are plenty of parking facilities. Alternatively, take public transport to a nearby station, and then a bus.

🚉 Chingford

🚌 20

Limited ♿

🅿 car parks

Free

Hainault Forest Country Park

Romford Road, Chigwell, Essex

This 364-hectare (900-acre) country park lies on the outer edges of London and combines woodland, farmland, a golf course, sports grounds and a fishing lake. The main feature of the park is a large wood, part of the Forest of Hainault which once belonged to the Abbey of Barking. Saved from total destruction at the end of the nineteenth century, the wood is full of ancient woodland species, such as crab apple and wild service. There is also plenty of open space to enjoy, with regular activities for children and walks for all the family organized by the park office (0181 500 7353).

θ Hainault, then bus

🚌 150, 247

Limited ♿

Free

Lee Valley Regional Park

Lee Valley Countryside Centre, Abbey Gardens, Waltham Abbey, Essex
(01992 713838)

The Lee Valley Park stretches north along 37 kilometres (23 miles) of the River Lea, from Stratford, East London, to Ware in Hertfordshire and was the first regional park in Britain to be created specifically as a centre for sporting and leisure activities and for nature conservation.

A good starting point is the Lee Valley Park Countryside Centre at Waltham Abbey. Here, a wealth of information guides and booklets are available to help you get more out of your visit. There is also a fascinating exhibition on the development of the valley from a peaceful backwater to a major industrial centre and its eventual return to a peaceful haven.

Within the 4,047 hectares (10,000 acres) of London's largest leisure park there are dozens of different activities to enjoy, from camping, orienteering, riding and angling to ice hockey, tennis and, of course, walking. The waterways play an important role here too – the main watersports centre is at Chingford (phone 0181 531 1129).

The park is a wonderful countryside and wildlife oasis, especially the further north you go. There are a number of bird and nature reserves, farms, country park areas and gardens, as well as acres of woodlands, meadows and open spaces to explore with plenty of places to stop and have a picnic.

You can follow one of the park's self-guided walks. Leaflets are available from the centre.

1. Fishers Green

There are two self-guided walks to follow here, which take you through a series of large lakes, meadow and woodland. Starting points along the walk include Cadmore Lane, Windmill Lane, Highbridge Street, Abbeyview and Crooked Mile.

2. River Lea Navigation Towpath

The towpath runs almost the full length of the valley.

3. Bowyers Water Circular Walks

From Hooks Marsh car park

There are several footpaths across Waltham Marsh (leading to Waltham Hall) to follow.

The centre also organizes regular countryside events, such as the Discovery festival for people with disabilities and the popular winter 'Birdwatch', phone for up-to-date events lists.

🚇 Waltham Cross (for Lee Valley Park Countryside Centre)

🚌 279, 317

Limited ♿

Open: Park: most sites daily, dawn – dusk; Countryside Centre: summer, daily, 10.00 a.m.–5.00 p.m.; winter, Tuesday–Sunday, 10.30 a.m.–4.00 p.m.

£ for some activities

Victoria Park

Hackney, E2

Although named after the queen, Victoria Park was the first London park to be opened for the public rather than for royalty. It has a small animal enclosure, where deer happily live alongside rabbits and guinea pigs. There is also a One o'Clock club (see page 138) and a playground, plus various sporting facilities for older children.

🚇 Cambridge Heath

🚌 8, 277

Free

NORTH

Alexandra Park and Palace

N22

A popular venue for outdoor pop, jazz and classical concerts, this is one of the largest open spaces in north London with fantastic views across the city from its highest points.

A wide range of sporting facilities is available here, including an artificial ski slope, football pitches, a cricket ground, playing fields, ice rink and pitch-and-putt golf course. Behind the palace (which is open as an exhibition and leisure centre), is a boating lake. For children there are playgrounds and an animal enclosure.

⊖ Wood Green

🔲 Alexandra Palace

🚌 W3

Limited ♿

Open: 24 hours, daily

Free

Clissold Park

Green Lanes, Stoke Newington, N16

Originally attached to a private home, Clissold Park has managed to retain many features of a small country estate, with acres of rolling parkland, home to a herd of fallow deer, and formal gardens. Other features of the park are the two ornamental lakes and an aviary. For children there is also a playground, paddling pool and One o'Clock club (see page 138). Sporting facilities include a bowling green, football pitch, netball and tennis courts, and running track.

⊖ Manor House.

🚌 141, 171A

♿ (There is an Easirider, a unique vehicle, which enables wheelchair users to have full access to the park. Contact Access to Leisure, Shoreditch Town Hall, 380 Old Street, EC1 (0171 739 7600 ext. 2316)

Free

Fryent Country Park

Fryent Way, Kingsbury, NW9

Fryent Country Park provides 121 hectares (300 acres) of woodland, hay meadows, open spaces, old ponds and hedgerows dating from medieval times. You can either explore the area alone or try one of the monthly guided walks given by Brent Countryside Rangers. If you would like to help in preserving and enhancing Fryent Country Park, Friends of Fryent Country Park and Barn Hill Conservation Group run a wide variety of conservation projects (0181 900 5038).

⊖ Kingsbury, Wembley Park

🔲 Kenton

🚌 PR2, 83, 302

Limited ♿

Free

Golders Hill Park

Golders Hill, NW11

Colourful flamingos live on a small lake near the flower garden. Elsewhere, in an enclosure, you can see deer, wallabies, goats and exotic birds such as the Sarus crane.

⊖ Golders Green

🚌 13, 28, 82, 210, 268

Free

Hampstead Heath

Hampstead, NW3

Hampstead Heath is probably the most famous open space in London. Its colourful history includes its role as a regular haunt of the highwayman Dick Turpin, while in 1763, Jackson, another highwayman, was hanged for highway murder behind Jack Straw's Castle. Parliament Hill (excellent for kite-flying) earned its name in several possible ways. Some believe that a Saxon folk-moot (an early version of Parliament) may have met there, while others claim that Guy Fawkes and his associates planned to watch Parliament burning from here.

Today the Heath covers some 319 hectares (789 acres) of woodland and meadows with splendid views of the city. It has many miles of heathland, meadows, hills, woods and ponds to explore, and people come here regularly to get to know it really well. The most popular areas are round Kenwood House at the north end of the Heath and Parliament Hill, which gives a panoramic view across London.

For refreshment, cafés can be found at Golders Hill (see page 156), Parliament Hill and Kenwood (see page 157) and for children there are two playgrounds and a One o'Clock Club. Sports facilities include an athletic track at Parliament Hill, bowling greens, cricket pitches, facilities for cross-country races and training, fishing on six ponds, football pitches, golf and putting, horse riding, model boating, orienteering, swimming in the lido and bathing ponds and tennis courts.

⊖ Belsize Park, Hampstead

🚇 Hampstead Heath

🚌 210, 268

Limited ♿

Free

Primrose Hill

Prince Albert Road, NW1

Primrose Hill lies to the north of Regent's Park, across Prince Albert Road, and is a marvellous place for kite-flying (see also page 87). From the top of the hill (64 metres/209 feet high), the view is breathtaking too so it is well worth the effort of walking up.

⊖ Chalk Farm

🚇 Primrose Hill

🚌 274

♿

Free

❖

Queen's Park

Kilburn, NW6

In 12 hectares (30 acres), Queen's Park packs in a good range of activities for all interests, as well as plenty of open space to walk and enjoy. In the summer, special entertainments, such as parties, games and activity days, are laid on for children, and the paddling pool is open then too. There are also playgrounds, which can be used all year round. Other facilities include a bandstand, and for sports enthusiasts, there are tennis courts, and a golf pitch-and-putt course.

⊖ Queen's Park

🚇 Brondesbury Park, Queen's Park

🚌 6, 36, 46, 206 (Monday–Saturday, not evenings)

♿

Free

Trent Park Country Park

Cockfosters Road, Enfield, Hertfordshire

This is a popular country park with masses to enjoy – such as a nature trail, ponds, public golf course and designated picnic areas – all set in 167 hectares (413 acres) of grasslands, woodland and lakes. In the centre of the park is the campus of Middlesex University, which uses the eighteenth-century house as the main college building.

There is also a special trail for blind or partially-sighted people; a tapping rail is provided from the main entrance on Cockfosters Road and Braille notices describe the scenery. Remember to bring some cash though, as there is a charge to use the car park.

⊖ Cockfosters, Oakwood

🚌 121, 298, 299, 307

Limited ♿

P Car park

Open: daily, 7.30 a.m.–30 minutes before sunset

£ (for car park)

SOUTH

Abbey Wood, Bostall Heath and Woods and Lesnes Abbey Woods

Bexley, SE2

This is the largest area of woodland in South London, and includes the site of the ruins of the twelfth-century Lesnes Abbey. The land is rugged and varied and the area is also rich in fossils. Permission to dig or sift for fossils can be obtained only from the park manager. There is also a pond which provides a refuge for wildlife and a café for refreshment. Sports facilities include a bowling green, cricket practice nets, a permanent orienteering course and a camping site (open all year, phone 0181 310 2233).

🚇 Abbey Wood

🚌 99, 229, 469

Limited ♿

Free

Battersea Park

Prince of Wales's Drive, SW11

Battersea is the second park to have been specifically created for Londoners rather than royalty (the first is Victoria Park in the East End) and is one of the most enjoyable for children. One of its main attractions is a children's zoo (see page 107). Other points of interest include the deer enclosure, which is now also home for a community of wallabies, as well as a colourful collection of peacocks, cranes and guinea fowl and the Victorian ornamental boating lake in the centre of the park.

The park has an outstanding collection of exotic trees, such as the tallest known black walnut, 33.5 metres (110 feet) high, a strawberry, a Kentucky coffee and a foxglove tree and you can follow a special tree trail, introducing all the different varieties.

The park also has London's largest adventure playground (see page 122) and a One o'Clock club (see page 138). Sports facilities include over twenty tennis courts, an athletics track, trim trail, bowling green and all-weather sports pitches.

⊖ Sloane Square, then bus

▣ Battersea Park, Queenstown Road

🚌 44, 137 (Monday–Saturday, not evenings), 137A (Monday–Friday, peak hours and Sundays), 344

&

Free

Burgess Park

Albany Road, SE5

Initially, Burgess Park was a small strip of land 6 hectares (15 acres) in size, known as Camberwell Open Space. From this original conception in the 1940s, the park has grown into one of the largest parks in south London. It includes a wealth of facilities for children and adults, with new developments under construction all the time. One of the most original features is a multi-cultural garden, with plants from tropical countries. There is also an attractive tree walk to follow, which points out some of London's most exotic trees, such as the Himalayan birch, the dawn redwood and the swamp cypress.

Other facilities include a lake, football pitches and tennis courts, a café and a playground.

⊖ Elephant & Castle, then bus

🚌 P3, 42

&

Free

Crystal Palace Park

Anerley Road, Crystal Palace, SE20

The dinosaurs in this Victorian theme park are still a favourite with children. Not far behind in popularity is the mix of city farm and the zoo. The mini fair, mini steam train and pony and trap are also favourites with children. The maze is still surrounded by the original ring of trees from the 1890s, and there is a concert bowl where Sunday evening concerts are given in summer. The National Sports Centre is also in the park.

The park also includes a museum, café and bandstand, where concerts are regularly performed during the summer. Sporting facilities include a cricket pitch and tennis courts and there are also facilities for orienteering, boating and fishing. Camping facilities are available too all year around; phone 0181 778 7155.

🚇 Crystal Palace

🚌 157, 176

♿

P

Free

Horniman Gardens

Forest Hill, SE23

At one end of these gardens is a small zoo, with a selection of goats, rabbits and turkeys, as well as a number of caged birds.

🚇 Forest Hill

🚌 P4, 63, 176, 185, 312

♿

Free

Morden Hall Park

Morden Hall Road, Morden, Surrey (0181 648 1845)

This extensive National Trust park is in the heart of Morden town centre and features several historic houses, including a seventeenth-century manor house, Morden Hall. Morden Cottage, a Gothic-style weatherboarded house, with a waterwheel, dairies, stables and rose gardens, was the site of snuff milling during the last century. Today, the mill is an environmental centre, used by school education groups. The park also contains a riverside café and a garden centre.

⊖ Morden

🚇 Morden Road

🚌 80, 118, 154, 157, 163

Limited ♿

Open: daily, 10.00 a.m.–5.00 p.m.; closed 25–26 December and 1 January

Free

Oxleas Wood, Castle Wood, Jackwood and Shepherdleas Woods

Falconwood, SE18

These woodlands and heathlands form part of the Green Chain, a chain of open spaces extending 25 kilometres (15 miles) from the Thames Barrier and Thamesmead through to Cator Park, New Beckenham. The oldest parts are Oxleas and Shepherdleas Wood, which can be traced right back to the end of the last Ice Age! The woodland contains a rich mixture of trees, shrubs and plants. There is a pattern of paths crisscrossing the woods and at the western end is

Severndroog Castle, an eighteenth-century folly, built for Sir William James of Eltham Park in 1784. The plaque above the entrance explains that the tower commemorates the conquest of the Castle of Severndroog on the coast of Malabar in 1755.

🚉 Eltham Park, Falconwood

🚌 B16, 89

Limited ♿

Free

Wandsworth Common

Trinity Road, SW17, and Bolingbroke Grove, SW11

Wandsworth Common is an important centre for wildlife and the common's Nature Study Centre is a good starting point for information (*Open:* Wednesday and Friday, 2.00 p.m.–4.00 p.m. and Sunday, 1.00 p.m.–4.00p.m.). 'The Scope' is probably the most interesting part of the common for wildlife; an area of 10 hectares (25 acres) between Trinity Road and Lyfor Road, there has been a policy here of minimal management to create an ecologically rich area.

Now a mixture of developing scrub and grasslands, 'The Scope' has colourful wild flowers from spring to autumn and provides a home for many animals and insects, including butterflies, frogs and warblers. Children's facilities include the Lady Allen playground, One o'Clock clubs, and other playgrounds. For sports enthusiasts there is angling (members only), tennis courts, cricket pitches, bowling green, football pitches and a trim trail.

🚉 Wandsworth Common

🚌 77, 91, 219

Limited ♿

[P]

Free

WEST

Bayhurst Wood Country Park and Ruislip Woods

Brakespear Road North, Harefield (01895 630078: Park Office; 01895 50111 ext. 2450: Hillingdon Leisure Services, Buckinghamshire)

Bayhurst is part of the Colne Valley Park; to the east, the wood is linked by footpaths through Mad Bess Park Wood, Copse Wood and Ruislip Common to Ruislip Lido and Park Wood, which together form an extensive stretch of public woodland and water covering some 307.5 hectares (760 acres).

The main feature of the park is an open-air woodland craft museum where you can learn some new skills, such as basket-making and weaving, at the special crafts demonstrations (by prior arrangement only). There are also plenty of picnic sites, bridleways and nature trails to explore: pick up details at the information centre. There is a café too (open in summer only).

⊖ Ruislip, then bus

🚌 331

Limited ♿

Free

Brent River Park

Ealing, Hanwell and Brentford
(0181 566 1929: Park Ranger)

This chain of green spaces stretches along the banks of the River Brent, with woodland walks, blackberries and the unusual canal 'staircase' of Hanwell's flight of locks. Part of the chain is a 1.2 hectare (3-acre) ancient woodland, Longwood, particularly interesting for birds and wild flowers, with a clean stream. There is a board walk to help access over parts of the wet woodland.

Children love the unusual menagerie in this park where they can see donkeys, wallabies, sheep, rabbits, squirrels and guinea pigs. In an inside enclosure there are marmosets and monkeys, as well as a reptile section with lizards and scorpions and also a piranha tank.

Details of five interesting circular walks are available from Brent River Park Environmental Centre, Brent Lodge Park, Church Road, W7.

⊖ Perivale
🚇 Hanwell, South Greenford
🚌 E8, 92, 195, 207, 282
♿

Open: Park: permanently; Environmental Centre: please phone for details
Free

Holland Park

Holland Park Road and Kensington High Street, Kensington W8
See also page 122

At the wooded, northern end of the park is a penned-off enclosure. Entry is not allowed, but from the path outside, you can see peacocks, peafowl, pheasants, rabbits and squirrels.

⊖ High Street Kensington, Holland Park
🚌 9, 10, 27, 28, 94
♿
Free

One o'Clock Clubs

Aimed at pre-school children, these clubs are run by local authorities in many parks. They are fully staffed and provide a range of activities, both inside the clubhouse, such as paintings and looking at picture books, and outside, on swings and slides. Children must be accompanied by adults at all times.

❖

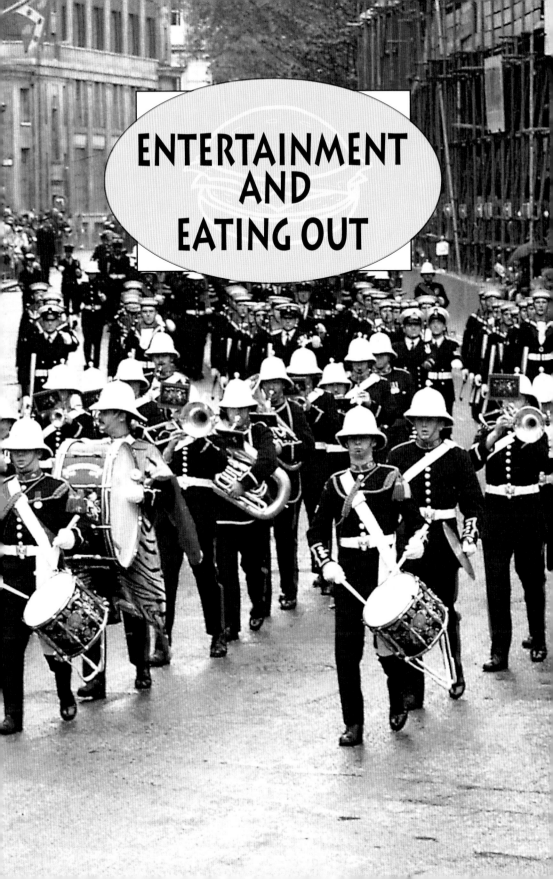

ENTERTAINMENT
AND
EATING OUT

WHAT'S ON –
THEATRES, CINEMAS AND CONCERTS

THEATRE

Children in London have an excellent choice of theatrical entertainment. London is probably the world centre for pantomime and some of television and film's biggest stars appear in shows across the West End and locally all through the Christmas season. Puppet theatre is usually popular with children and there are several good puppet theatres in London. Many of the smaller theatres, such as the Polka Theatre, the Tricycle Theatre and the Unicorn Arts Theatre, regularly stage shows for children of a very high standard. Children's shows are also held less frequently at the Lyric Hammersmith, the Riverside Studios, Royal National Theatre and Sadler's Wells. There are also about sixty touring children's theatre companies that perform in venues throughout London. The Barbican Centre holds regular weekend festivals and fun days for all the family too.

Don't underestimate the ability of children to enjoy 'grown-up' drama, though. Musicals are generally popular and it is worth trying something a little stronger, such as Shakespeare, if children are interested – by taking plays out of the classroom, they are far more likely to enjoy drama.

Open-air Children's Theatre

Free theatrical performances for children are given regularly during the summer holidays in these venues:

Bushy Park, Hampton, Surrey (0181 979 1586)

Greenwich Park, SE10 (0181 858 2608)

Hampstead Heath, NW3 (0181 348 9908)

Kensington Gardens, W8 (0181 298 2100)

Regent's Park, NW1 (0171 486 7905)

Richmond Park, Richmond, Surrey (0181 948 3209)

Battersea Arts Centre

Old Town Hall, Lavender Hill, SW11
(0171 223 2223: box office)
See also pages 43 and 60
Special shows for younger children are held on
Saturdays, including puppet performances –
BAC is the home of the Puppet Centre Trust.

🚇 Clapham Junction
🚌 77, 77A
♿

Open: 10 a.m.–9.00 p.m. (Monday, to 6.00 p.m.)
£–££

Little Angel Theatre

14 Dagmar Passage, Cross Street, Islington, N1 (0171 226 1787: box office)
Children aged three and upwards are catered for at the Little Angel. On Saturdays
and Sundays there are two shows – at 11 a.m. and 3.00 p.m. – with the occasional
evening show. The theatre also puts on extra shows during half-terms and most
holidays. The work presented covers a wide range of puppetry from many
cultures, both the Little Angel's own work and that of visiting companies. It can
be anything from a traditional folk story to a Christmas pantomime. The theatre
is also developing puppet work to present to adults.

⊖ Angel
🚇 Essex Road
🚌 4, 19, 30, 43, 73
♿
£–££

London Bubble Theatre Company

3 Elephant Lane, Rotherhithe, SE16 (0171 237 4434)
Any open space large enough for their 'bubble' tent becomes a temporary home
for this threatre company, the only fully mobile one in Britain. The company
tours the parks of London every summer, spending about two weeks at every
location. Its touring plays are aimed at under-elevens, but it also has two youth
theatres, for fourteen- to twenty-five-year-olds in Southwark and for twelve- to
sixteen-year-olds in Bexley.

Movingstage Marionette Company

Puppet Theatre Barge, Blomfield Road, Little Venice, W9 (0171 249 6876: box office)
Water and marionettes work in harmony together at the Movingstage Marionette
Company. Based in an old working barge on a pretty backwater of the Regent's
Canal, the Puppet Theatre Barge is an unusual and fascinating theatre for both
children and adults.

Plays and poems are selected from existing works and occasionally new work is
commissioned from contemporary playwrights and poets. During the winter the

Company develops ideas for its productions and carves the marionettes as well as performing regularly for the public from November to May at its Little Venice base. The shows are toured up and down the Thames between Oxford and Richmond in the barge during the summer.

θ Warwick Avenue

🚌 6, 18, 46

No ♿

£–££

Polka Theatre for Children

240 The Broadway, Wimbledon, SW19 (0181 543 4888)

See also page 44

The Polka Theatre is the only theatre entirely devoted to children in London and has two shows daily for families and schools in its two theatre spaces. Shows vary from plays to mime and music and are suitable for children of all ages. As well as the main theatre, there are exhibitions of past productions, an adventure room (a theatre space), a workshop and café. In the shop there is a special selection of souvenirs affordable with pocket money.

θ South Wimbledon, Wimbledon

🚆 Wimbledon

🚌 57, 93, 155

♿ (main theatre)

£–££

Tricycle Theatre

269 Kilburn High Road, Kilburn, NW6 (0171 328 1000)

See also page 42

The Tricycle has a great reputation for presenting innovative theatre for children – from drama and musicals to puppetry, magic and clowning – so try to book seats well in advance. Children under seven must be accompanied by an adult. The shows are given every Saturday between September and June at 11.30 a.m. and 2.00 p.m. Each show is aimed at a particular age range but most are for children aged from three to seven. There are regular visits from a variety of performers including solo clown acts and large-scale touring theatre companies. A children's menu is available in the café.

⊖ Kilburn
🚆 Brondesbury
🚌 16, 16A, 32
♿
£

Unicorn Arts Theatre

6 Great Newport Street, WC2 (0171 836 3334: box office)
See also page 38

Founded in 1947, the Unicorn is the oldest professional children's theatre in London and aims to introduce live theatre to all children and promote their enjoyment of it. A season of about six plays for varied age groups is presented from September to June. From Tuesday to Friday, the company performs for school groups, but at weekends the theatre is open to the general public. Performances are given on Saturday at 11.00 a.m. and at 2.30 p.m. and on Sunday at 2.30 p.m.

⊖ Leicester Square
🚌 24, 29, 176
♿
£–££

Waterman's Arts Centre

40 High Street, Brentford, Middlesex (0181 568 1176: box office)
See also page 47

A regular Saturday afternoon theatre performance for over-threes is held here, starting at 2.30 p.m. Shows vary from magic and music to puppet shows.

⊖ Gunnersbury, then bus
🚆 Kew Bridge
🚌 65, 237, 267
♿
£–££

CINEMAS

Most of the cinemas in the West End are owned by a handful of international companies and generally show the latest blockbusters. Leicester Square lies at the heat of London's movie kingdom, with four top cinemas: the MGM, the Empire, the Odeon and the Warner West End. These cinemas are often the venues for celebrity and royal premieres, where the stars of the latest film come to rub shoulders with their famous friends.

Cinema programmes generally change over every one to three weeks – keep an eye out in the *Evening Standard* or *Time Out* and other listings magazine for new openings. New films for children are always released to coincide with half-terms and holidays, but many cinemas in London also screen both new and classic children's films at other times. Some cinemas have children's film clubs, which also hold competitions and events. Tickets for these cinemas are usually reasonably inexpensive. Remember too that many West End cinemas have half-price tickets for under-fourteens.

Included below is a selection of cinemas with the most to offer children.

Barbican Splodge Club

Barbican Centre, EC2 (0171 638 8891: box office)
See also page 39
The Splodge club is a multi-activity scheme for children. The Children's Cinema Club shows films on Saturday afternoons – phone for programme details.
⊖ Barbican
🚌 4 (Monday–Saturday), 56
♿
£

Clapham Picture House

Venn Street, SW4 (0171 498 2242: recorded information; 0171 498 3323: box office)
Children's films are shown on Saturday mornings and during school holidays.
⊖ Clapham Common
🚌 35, 37, 60, 88, 155
No ♿
£

National Film Theatre

South Bank, SE1 (0171 928 3232: box office)
The National Film Theatre regularly puts on films for children, particularly during school holidays. Times and dates will vary.
⊖/🚆 Waterloo
🚌 26, 68, 168, 171, 188
♿
£

Phoenix Cinema

High Road, Finchley, N2 (0181 883 2233: recorded information)
The Saturday Kids Club shows a range of classic and new children's films every week.
⊖ East Finchley
🚌 263
Limited ♿
£

Rio Dalston

107 Kingsland High Street, Hackney, E8
(0171 249 2722)

The Saturday Morning Picture Club presents a children's feature film every week. By buying an admission ticket, you automatically become a member of the club for free. There are generous incentives for members – for example, if you watch five films, the sixth is free.

🚇 Dalston, Kingsland
🚌 30, 56, 67, 149
♿
£

Virgin Hammersmith

King Street, W6 (0181 748 0557: recorded information)
This cinema also has a Young Lion Kids Club that puts on films for children and accompanying adults every Saturday morning.

⊖ Hammersmith
🚌 27, 190, 267, 391
No ♿
£

CONCERTS

Ernest Read Concerts for Children

(0181 942 0318)

For over fifty years, Ernest Read concerts have been performed to children across the country. In London the concerts take place in several venues, including the Royal Albert Hall and the Royal Festival Hall (phone the above number for information about forthcoming concerts). Children do not have a chance to become bored at these concerts as there is plenty of opportunity for audience participation and the conductor allows for 'fidgeting' time between pieces. Even the concert programmes are specially aimed at children, with cartoons, quizzes and competitions to keep them entertained.

London Symphony Orchestra Family Concerts

Barbican Centre, Silk Street, EC21 (0171 638 8891: box office)
This orchestra holds occasional concerts for children, which involve audience participation. Recommended ages are seven to twelve. Phone to find out about forthcoming events.

⊖ Barbican
🚌 4 (Monday–Saturday), 56
♿
£–££

FOOD FOR KIDS

WHETHER you fancy a trip to Planet Hollywood in Leicester Square or want to get your fingers sticky in Kensington or simply settle for a pizza, London's wealth of good eating places means you are unlikely to run out of somewhere special to take the children.

In general, Sunday lunch-times are the best times to eat out. There is a party atmosphere in many places, with balloons, clowns and even face-painting sometimes available. Many of the restaurants featured here make ideal venues for your own parties at any time – and have the added advantage that there is no clearing up to do afterwards.

Although Smollensky's, the Hard Rock Café and other themed family restaurants are great fun as a special treat, don't forget about less expensive alternatives. Italian restaurants are always very friendly towards children and Chinese restaurants are a good choice too – children like the variety of small portions.

If you don't want a long sit-down meal, then try some of the best fast food places in town (see page 154) or indulge at some of the ice-cream parlours that are popping up all over London. Some pubs have gardens where children are welcome, particularly in summer time.

RESTAURANTS

The Blue Elephant

4–6 Fulham Broadway, SW6 (0171 385 6595)

Thai food can be expensive, but on Sunday lunch-times at the Blue Elephant, the younger you are, the less you pay. There are three price bands: aged under six years, seven to ten and ten to fifteen – while adults pay a fixed price however much they eat.

⊖ Fulham Broadway

🚍 14, 28, 211, 295

♿

Open: Monday–Friday, 12 noon–3.00 p.m.; Monday–Saturday, 7.00 p.m.–11.00 p.m.; Sunday, 12 noon–3.30 p.m.

££

Deals

Chelsea Harbour, SW10 (0171 795 1001)
14–16 Foubert's Place, W1 (0171 287 1001)
Bradmore House, Hammersmith Broadway, W6 (0181 563 1001)

Armed with a royal pedigree (two of the restaurant's owners are Lord Lichfield and Viscount Linley) and a refreshingly enthusiastic approach to creating a fun burger restaurant, Deals opened first in Chelsea Harbour. Since then it has opened two more branches, which are proving equally popular.

Sunday lunch-times are the best time to come with children, and treats include face-painting and magicians, 'bottomless Coke' (as much as you can drink for a set price) and a chance to create an ice-cream pudding from the selection of flavours on the pudding trolley.

⊖ Oxford Circus (W1); Hammersmith (Hammersmith); Earl's Court, Fulham Broadway, Sloane Square, then bus (Chelsea Harbour)

🚌 3, 6, 12, 15, 25 (W1); 9, 10, 27, 211, 266 (Hammersmith); 11, 22, 31, 211 (Chelsea Harbour)

&. (all branches)

Open: Chelsea Harbour: daily, 11.00 am–12 midnight (Sunday, to 11.15 p.m.); Foubert's Place: Monday–Saturday, 12 noon–11 p.m. (Friday and Saturday, to 1 a.m.), closed Sunday; Hammersmith: Monday–Thursday, 12 noon–3.00 p.m. and 5.00–11.00 p.m.; Friday–Sunday, 12 noon–11.00 p.m.

££

Hard Rock Café

150 Old Park Lane, W1 (0171 629 0382)

Its queues are legendary, but it is surprising how quickly you can get inside and sit down. While Planet Hollywood celebrates the movies, the theme at the Hard Rock café is rock and roll. The idea for this began when Eric Clapton personally donated a guitar which was swiftly followed by another from Pete Townshend. The memorabilia collection now numbers over 22,000 items which are regularly rotated around the world.

On the food front, vegetarians are particularly well served, with a special menu devised by Linda McCartney.

θ Hyde Park Corner

🚌 10, 16, 36, 73, 82

♿

Open: daily, 11.00 a.m.–11.00 p.m.

££

Pizza Express

With plenty of balloons to chase around the restaurant and friendly staff who happily dodge both children and balloons, the numerous branches of Pizza Express are ideal places to go with children who want to let off steam and adults who want a decent pizza.

Central London branches at:

133 Baker Street, NW1 (0171 486 0888)

21 Barrett Street W1 (0171 629 1001)

9 Bow Street, WC2 (0171 240 3443)

The Colonnades, 26 Porchester Square, W2 (0171 229 7784)

30 Coptic Street, Bloomsbury, WC1 (0171 636 3232)

15 Gloucester Road, SW7 (0171 584 9078)

11 Knightsbridge, SW1 (0171 235 5550)

29 Romilly Street, W1 (0171 734 6112)

154 Victoria Street, SW1 (0171 828 1477)

29 Wardour Street, W1 (0171 437 7215)

♿ (most branches)

Open: times vary

£–££

Planet Hollywood

13 Coventry Street, W1 (0171 287 1000)

Inspired by the world of the movies, Planet Hollywood cleverly sells a slice of glamour to the public, along with their burgers and fries. A worldwide restaurant chain, partly owned by such top film stars as Sylvester Stallone and Bruce Willis, each venue is packed with dozens of props and costumes from famous movies.

What makes these restaurants particularly special is that you are allowed to touch the pieces too – among the most exciting items at the London branch are Harrison Ford's whip from *Indiana Jones and the Last Crusade*, Charlie Chaplin's hat and cane, and the Terminator Cyborg from *Terminator 2*. In addition to the memorabilia there is a handprint wall which displays the palms of some of the world's most famous film stars, including Clint Eastwood, Kevin Costner and Johnny Depp.

θ Piccadilly Circus

🚌 3, 12, 14, 19, 22, 38

♿

Open: daily, 11.00 a.m.–11.00 p.m.

££

Rock Garden

6–7 The Piazza, Covent Garden, WC2 (0171 836 4052)
With its outdoor tables offering great views of the comings and goings in Covent
Garden Piazza, the Rock Garden is a popular summertime restaurant. The menu
is basic – burgers and more burgers – but this shouldn't put you off. It can get very
busy, though, so you may have to queue for a long time for a table.
 Covent Garden
 6, 11, 15, 24, 29

Open: daily, 11.00 a.m.–midnight; Friday and Saturday, to 1.00 a.m.
£–££

Rock Island Diner

Second Floor, London Pavilion, WC1 (0171 287 5500)
Come here between 12 noon and 5.00 p.m. on Saturday and Sunday and children
can eat for free! This, in addition to its lively atmosphere and good food, make the
Rock Island one of the better American theme restaurants in London. You can
pop in after a visit to the Rock Circus (see page 60) or the Pepsi Trocadero (see
page 35).
 Piccadilly Circus
 3, 12, 14, 19, 38

Open: daily, 11.00 a.m.–11.30 p.m.
££

Smollensky's Balloon

1 Dover Street, W1 (0171 491 1199)
105 Strand, WC2 (0171 497 2101)
Lively restaurants with loads of entertainment for children, from jesters, clowns and
Nintendo machines to puppets, magic
shows, face-painting and story tellers –
entertainments for kids take place on
Saturday and Sunday afternoons from 1.00
p.m. to 3.00 p.m.

 The menu includes all the favourites
from steak to burgers and wonderful
puddings if you still have room.
 Covent Garden, Embankment
(Strand); Green Park (Dover Street)
 6, 9, 11, 15, 23 (Strand); 9, 14, 19,
22, 38 (Dover Street)

Open: daily, 12 noon–12 midnight; Sunday,
to 10.30 p.m.;
££

Sticky Fingers

1a Phillimore Gardens, W8 (0171 938 5338)

Owned by ex-Rolling Stone Bill Wyman, this is one of the most enjoyable restaurants in London. Don't forget to book in advance for Sunday lunch and be sure to turn up promptly. The menu is mainly burger-based, with a few vegetarian options, and the interest comes from the goodies available for children.

Colouring books are handed out to children so they don't get bored during mealtimes and they can take part in a Draw Your Waiter competition. Wonderful balloons are given as freebies too – with lots of different shapes, from helicopters and fishing rods to fish and flowers.

⊖ High Street Kensington

🚌 9, 10, 27, 28, 31

♿

Open: daily, 12 noon–11.30 p.m.

££

TGI Friday's

6 Bedford Street, WC2 (0171 379 0585)

Branches at:

96–98 Bishops Bridge Road, W2 (0171 229 8600)

25–29 Coventry Street, W1 (0171 839 6262)

Enfield Retail Park, Great Cambridge Road, Enfield (0181 363 5200)

701–704 Purley Way, Croydon, Surrey (0181 681 1313)

Unit 101 Bentall Centre, Wood Street, Kingston-upon-Thames, Surrey (0181 547 2900)

Watford Way, Mill Hill, NW7 (0181 203 9779)

The all-American experience of slick service, a colourful setting and huge helpings of favourite food combine to make a fun family restaurant. The VIP treatment for children includes a free balloon and a colouring book.

⊖ Charing Cross, Covent Garden, Embankment

🚆 Charing Cross

🚌 6, 9, 11, 15, 23

♿

Open: daily, 12.00 noon–11.30 p.m.

££

SNACKS

Bar Crêperie

21 South Row, WC2 (0171 836 2137)

Situated in the heart of busy Covent Garden, this is a great place for ringside seats to watch the buskers who perform close by.

⊖ Covent Garden

🚌 6, 9, 11, 15, 23

♿

Open: daily, 10.00 a.m.–11.30 p.m.

£–££

Baskin-Robbins

Ice-creams and doughnuts are available here.
There are a number of branches throughout
London which are good for a quick
pitstop, but the tables are not comfortable
enough for a long stay. The ice-creams
are also available at the Empire Cinema,
Leicester Square, and the Plaza
Cinema, Lower Regent Street.

Open: daily, 11.00 a.m.–11.00 p.m.
&

£

Canadian Muffin Company

9 Brewer Street, W1 (0171 287 3555)
Branches at:
2 Clarence Street, Kingston-upon-Thames, Surrey (0181 549 4432)
352 Fulham Road, SW10 (0171 351 0015)
13 Islington High Street, N1 (0171 833 5004)
5 King Street, WC2 (0171 379 1525)
A fresh muffin and a steaming cup of hot chocolate are great restoratives on a cold
winter's day. The cafés are wonderfully relaxed places for a weekend family break-
fast or just a tea-time snack.

θ Piccadilly Circus

🚌 3, 6, 19, 22, 23

&

Open: daily, 9.30 a.m.–6.30 p.m. (all branches)

£

Haagen-Dazs Ice-Cream Parlours

Leicester Square, WC2 (0171 287 9577)
Branches at:
226–230 Fulham Road, SW10 (0171 351 7706)
83 Gloucester Road, SW7 (0171 373 9988)
The Piazza, Covent Garden, WC2 (0171 240 0436)
88 Queensway, W2 (0171 229 0668)
Haagen-Dazs led the American ice-cream revolution in Britain in the 1980s and has since spawned
a number of competitors. But it is still holding
strong and at Haagen-Dazs ice-cream parlours
you can choose from many different flavours and
toppings.

θ Leicester Square

🚌 4, 19, 24, 29, 176

&

Open: daily, 10.00 a.m.–11.00 p.m.

£–££

Harrods Ice-Cream Parlour & Crêperie

4th Floor, Harrods, Knightsbridge, SW3 (0171 730 1234)

There is a mouthwatering selection of ice-cream sundaes, milkshakes and sweet and savoury crêpes to enjoy here after you have explored the toy department. If it is too busy, try the Georgian Restaurant on the same floor, which serves traditional lunches for adults with half-price meals for children under twelve.

⊖ Knightsbridge

🚌 10, 19, 52, 74, 137

♿

Open: store opening hours

£–££

Marine Ices

Haverstock Hill, Hampstead, NW3 (0171 485 3132)

People from all over London make a pilgrimage to this ice-cream parlour, which has about twenty flavours of sorbets and ice-creams.

⊖ Chalk Farm

🚌 168

♿

Open: Monday–Saturday, 10.30 a.m.–10.45 p.m.; Sunday, 11.00 a.m.–7.00 p.m.

£–££

FAST FOOD

Hamburgers and chips may not be top of an adult's list of healthy foods, but they have their place, particularly if you have your hands full of hungry children and don't want to spend too much money. Central London abounds with Burger Kings, McDonald's and other fast-food emporiums. The best-known ones close to places of interest that are featured in this book are listed below together with a couple of more unusual fast-food eateries. Finally, don't ignore the multitude of sandwich shops in London. Most offer good-quality, freshly prepared sandwiches and you can choose from a variety of fillings. Branches of the Pret à Manger chain are particularly recommended.

BURGERS & FRIES

Burger King
126–138 Camden High Street, NW1 (0171 482 4689)
27–29 Euston Road, NW1 (0171 837 6073)
17 Leicester Square, WC2 (0171 930 0158)
425–427 Oxford Street, W1 (0171 491 8551)
298 Regent Street, W1 (0171 580 5108)
1a–1b Tottenham Court Road, W1 (0171 323 6744)

KFC
128 Baker Street, W1 (0171 486 9769)
65 Brompton Road, SW3 (0171 584 6781)

1–2 Coventry Street, W1 (0171 287 2189)
542–544 Oxford Street, W1 (0171 724 2055)
75 Strand, WC2 (0171 497 3427)

McDonald's
57 Haymarket, SW1 (0171 930 9302)
112 High Holborn, WC1 (0171 404 0162)
49 King's Road, SW3 (0171 824 8133)
4 Marble Arch, W1 (0171 402 6297)
185 Oxford Street, W1 (0171 494 2347)
65 Shaftesbury Avenue, W1 (0171 287 8391)
68 St Martin's Lane, WC2 (0171 240 3096)
35 Strand, WC2 (0171 839 6086)
134 Tottenham Court Road, W1 (0171 888 9026)
8 Tower Hill, EC3 (0171 702 3115)
206–207 Whiteleys Centre, W2 (0171 221 2081)

WHOLEFOOD

Neal's Corner Sandwich Shop
1 Monmouth Street, WC2 (0171 836 2066)

Neal's Yard Soup and Salad Bar
2 Neal's Yard, WC2 (0171 836 3233)

PICNICS

Any park or green open space provides a site for a picnic. If you are using public transport to get there, plan the food carefully so that it is not too awkward or heavy to carry. You can usually find somewhere selling cold drinks near your chosen destination. A large variety of take-away food – ranging from sandwiches and rolls to individual trifles and flavoured yoghurts – is available in most super-markets. Don't forget to take a damp flannel to wipe sticky fingers and do make sure you leave no litter behind!

TEA ON THE LAWN AT *alexandra palace*

PARK CAFES

Most parks have refreshment facilities of some sort, even if it is just an ice-cream vendor, but some parks have cafés and restaurants which are so good that they are worth mentioning in their own right.

Clissold Park Café

The Mansion, Clissold Park, Stoke Newington, N16 (0181 800 1021)
In a Grade II listed building, this is a family-friendly cafe with plenty of hearty tea-time cakes and biscuits.
⊖ Manor House
🚌 141, 171A
♿
Open: daily, 10.00 a.m.–7.00 p.m.
£–££

Golders Hill Park Cafeteria

North End Way, Golders Hill, NW11 (0181 455 8010)
Just down the road from its big brother, Hampstead Heath, this small, but pleasant, park boasts its own bandstand and a delightful cafeteria run by an Italian family, who have decorated it with baskets and tubs of colourful flowers.
⊖ Golders Green
🚌 210, 268
♿
Open: daily, 10.30 a.m.–9.00 p.m.
£–££

❖

Ham House

Ham, Richmond, Surrey (0181 940 1950)

Set in an orchard in the grounds of the recently restored Ham House, this is a lovely setting to enjoy a light lunch or tea.

⊖/🚉 Richmond, then bus

🚌 65, 371

&

Open: Tuesday–Sunday, 10.00 a.m.–5.00 p.m.

£–££

Kenwood House Café

The Old Stables, Kenwood House, Hampstead Lane, NW3 (0181 348 1286)

There is a delightful café and restaurant in the beautiful old Coach House at Kenwood House, where you can have tea and snacks or a wholesome and filling lunch.

⊖ Archway, Golders Green, then bus

🚌 210

&

Open: May–September, daily, 10.00 a.m.–6.00 p.m.; October–April, daily, 10.00 a.m.–4.00 p.m.

£–££

Lauderdale House

Waterlow Park, Highgate Hill, N6 (0181 341 4807)

Lauderdale House, a restored Grade I listed building, now houses a small art gallery and a café. You can take your food out on to the terrace overlooking the park below.

⊖ Archway

🚌 143, 210, 271

&

Open: daily, 9.00 a.m.–6.00 p.m.

Pembroke Lodge

Richmond Park, Surrey (0181 940 8207)

Close to the Richmond entrance to the park, Pembroke Lodge offers snacks and afternoon tea in its own grounds within the park.

⊖/🚉 Richmond

🚌 65, 371

&

Open: March–October, daily, 10.00 a.m.–30 minutes before park closes; November–February, daily, 10.00 a.m.–4.00 p.m.

THE LONDON YEAR

OZENS of events take place in London throughout each year that are of interest to children. These range from the pomp and ceremony of Trooping the Colour in June to the colourful parades of the Notting Hill Carnival in August. Many events happen regularly at the same time each year. However, there are always new things going on. Keep an eye out in the listings magazines and the local press for half-term and holiday events taking place near you.

ROYAL CEREMONIAL EVENTS

The Mounting of the Guard

Horse Guards, Whitehall, SW1

The Mounting of the Guard takes place at the Horse Guards, opposite Whitehall, at 11.00 a.m. on weekdays and 10.00 a.m. on Sundays. The guard is formed from two units of the Household Cavalry – the Blues (identified by red plumes on their helmets) and the Life Guards (white-plumed).

⊖ Charing Cross, Westminster

▦ Charing Cross

🚌 11, 12, 24, 77A, 88

&

Free

The Changing of the Guard

Buckingham Palace, SW1

The Queen's Guard, usually formed from one of the regiments of Foot Guards (the Scots, Irish, Welsh, Coldstream and Grenadier) is changed daily at 11.30 a.m. The ceremony takes place inside the Palace railings and can be viewed by the public from outside. The Guard leaves Wellington Barracks at 11.27 a.m. and marches via Birdcage Walk to the Palace. Between early April and September the ceremony takes place daily; from September to April it occurs on alternate days.

⊖ Green Park, St James's Park, Victoria

▦ Victoria

🚌 11, 16, 24, 52, 73

&

Free

Horse Guards

Whitehall, SW1

The Queen's Life Guard is changed daily throughout the year at 11.00 a.m. from Monday to Saturday and at 10.00 a.m. on Sundays. The ceremony lasts about minutes. The Guard leaves Hyde Park Barracks at 10.28 a.m. (9.28 a.m. on Sunday) and rides via Hyde Park Corner, Constitution Hill and the Mall. Times may be different on days when state events are taking place. There is a short ceremonial dismounting of the mounted sentries every day at 4.00 p.m.

θ Charing Cross, Westminster
🚇 Charing Cross
🚌 11, 12, 24, 77A, 88
♿
Free

St James's Palace

Pall Mall, SW1

The St James's Palace detachment of the Queen's Guard marches to Buckingham Palace at 11.15 a.m. and returns to St James's Palace at 12.10 p.m. The Guard is changed only on the days when there is a Guard Change at Buckingham Palace.

θ Green Park, St James's Park
🚌 9, 14, 19, 22, 38
♿
Free

Gun Salutes

Gun salutes take place annually on the following dates, except if they fall on a Sunday, when they are fired on the following day:

    6 February Accession Day
    21 April Queen's birthday
    2 June Coronation Day
    10 June The Duke of Edinburgh's birthday
    4 August Queen Mother's birthday

On these days there is always a 41-gun salute at noon at Hyde Park, opposite the Dorchester Hotel in Park Lane, fired by the King's Troop, Royal Horse Artillery. The soldiers gallop their horses down the park, pulling the massive gun carriages behind them, set them up, then fire.

A 62-gun salute is fired at the Tower of London at 1.00 p.m. by the Honourable Artillery Company. Gun salutes also take place for Trooping the Colour and the State Opening of Parliament, as well as for some state visits – details for these vary.

Trooping the Colour: second Saturday in June

This colourful ceremony marks the official birthday of the Queen and takes place at Horse Guards Parade in Whitehall. Wearing the official uniform of one of the regiments of which she is Colonel-in-Chief, the Queen leaves the Palace at 10.30

a.m. to take the salute of the Brigade of Guards and the Household Cavalry. This is followed by a display of marching and the 'trooping' (display) of the 'colour' (or flag) of one of the regiments of Foot Guards.

The Queen returns to Buckingham Palace at 12.30 p.m. and appears on the balcony for a flypast by the RAF at 1.00 p.m., when there is another gun salute at the Tower of London.

If you want to have a good viewpoint on the Mall to watch the parade, you need to enter a ticket ballot for which there is a small charge. For details, write, by the end of February, to: The Brigade Major (Trooping the Colour), Household Division, Horse Guards Parade, SW1 enclosing a stamped addressed envelope. There is a maximum of two tickets per application.

⊖ Charing Cross, St James's Park

🚌 3, 11, 24, 53, 88

♿

Small charge for a position on the Mall

JANUARY/FEBRUARY

Lord Mayor of Westminster's New Year's Day Spectacular

This parade has been taking place for several years now and is a great way to start the year, with plenty to enjoy, from marching bands, floats and veteran cars to horse-drawn carriages and clowns.

The parade starts in Parliament Square at 12 noon and travels along Whitehall to Trafalgar Square, west along Cockspur Street and Pall Mall, north along Lower Regent Street to Piccadilly Circus, west along Piccadilly, north along Berkeley Street, finishing in Berkeley Square.

⊖ Westminster

🚌 3, 11, 24, 53, 77A

♿

Free

Chinese New Year Festival

Soho, WC2

London's Chinese community is based in Soho and the annual New Year celebration are the highlight of their year. As the Chinese calendar is lunar, the date varies between late January and early February.

The area around Gerrard Street is decorated with streamers and garlands. Young men, dressed in colourful, theatrical lion costumes, dance through the streets, receiving gifts of money and food from local restaurants, shops and residents.

Easter Parade

Battersea Park, SW11

A colourful carnival takes place on Easter Sunday. The parade starts at 3.00 p.m. but from 10.00 a.m. onwards there are many attractions, including a fairground and various stage acts.

🚌 Battersea Park, Queenstown Road

🚌 19, 44, 45A, 49, 137

♿

£

London Harness Horse Parade

Regent's Park, NW1

Judging of horses and carts, drays and brewers' vans is followed by a procession twice round the Inner Circle on Easter Monday morning.

⊖ Baker Street, Regent's Park

🚌 13, 27, 30, 82, 113, 274

♿

Free

London Marathon

(0171 222 8000: Sportsline)

Since the first London Marathon in 1980, this has become the world's largest road race, with over 35,000 starters. International runners lead the crowd and behind come a mixture of serious runners, joggers, celebrities and fancy dress fun runners, who all raise thousands of pounds for charity. No one under 18 years is allowed to participate, but you can be any age to enjoy spectating. The two best places to watch are at Greenwich, where it all starts at 9.30 a.m., and the finish at Westminster Bridge (approximately 12 noon). The runners all appreciate some moral support so you could just stand anywhere along the route and cheer them on!

Start: **DLR** Island Gardens (then via foot tunnel)

🚌 Greenwich

🚌 177, 180, 199

Finish: ⊖ Westminster

🚌 3, 12, 53, 109, 211

♿

Free

We're right on course for the Marathon

Sunday 18 April

We have all the best viewpoints for the London Marathon

Monument, Mansion House, Blackfriars, Embankment, Temple (open specially), St. James's Park, Waterloo (Shell exit) and Charing Cross stations are just a short walk (or run) from the action. Ideal for watching the exciting final stages of the race.

So take the Tube and be ahead of the field.

Runners, if it all gets too much, simply show your race number at the ticket barrier and we'll carry you to the tape free!

MAY

Punch and Judy Festival

St Paul's Churchyard, Covent Garden, WC2 (0171 240 2255)

An annual Punch and Judy Festival is held on the closest Sunday to 9 May to commemorate the date in 1662 when Samuel Pepys watched the first recorded Punch and Judy show.

❖

θ Covent Garden
🚌 6, 11, 15, 24, 29
♿
Free

Bank Holiday Weekend at the Barbican

Barbican Centre Foyer, Silk Street, EC2 (0171 638 8891)
Two days of special foyer and concert events are held during the May Day Bank
Holiday weekend. Modern and traditional jazz is often featured. Phone for details
of the programme.
θ Barbican
🚌 4 (Monday–Saturday), 56
♿

£ for concerts, foyer events are free

JUNE

Capital Radio

A season of weekend road shows begins in July and continues until September.
Shows take place in outdoor venues, such as major local parks and commons.
Tune in for details.
♿
Free

Beating the Retreat: Household Division

Horse Guards Parade, SW1
This is a popular military display of marching and drilling bands of the Household
Division. There are mounted bands, trumpeters, massed bands and pipes and
drums. The floodlit display begins at 9.30 p.m. Tickets are available from the end
of February from Premier Box Office, 1b Bridge Street, SW1 (opposite Big Ben).
θ St James's Park
🚌 11, 24, 211
♿
££

Sounding the Retreat: Light Division

Horse Guards Parade, SW1
Later in the month is Sounding the Retreat: Light Division, with massed band
displays. Performances usually start at 7.30 p.m. and tickets are available by post
from Headquarters, The Light Division, Sir John Moore Barracks, Winchester,
SO22 6NQ.
θ St James's Park
🚌 11, 24, 211
♿
£

Royal Tournament

Earl's Court, Warwick Road, SW5
(0171 373 8141: box office)
Members of the armed forces demonstrate
their versatile skills in this popular spectacle.
They also take part in re-enactments of
historical events.

⊖ Earl's Court
🚌 C1, 31, 74
♿
££

Royal International Horse Show

Wembley Arena, Stadium Way, Wembley, Middlesex
(0181 900 1234: box office)
The superb displays of horsemanship make this a
special event for dedicated young riders.

⊖ Wembley Central, Wembley Park
🚉 Wembley Central, Wembley Stadium
🚌 18, 83, 92, 182, 224
♿
££

Doggett's Coat and Badge Race

0171 332 1456 (information)
Six Thames watermen row against the tide from London Bridge to Chelsea
Bridge in late July or early August, and the winner is presented with a scarlet coat
with silver buttons and a badge. This is the oldest rowing event in the world, insti-
tuted in about 1715.

⊖/🚉 London Bridge (for start of race), Sloane Square (for finish of race)
🚌 22A, 35, 40, 47, 133 (to London Bridge, for start); 11, 137
(Monday–Saturday, not evenings); 211 (to Chelsea Bridge, for finish)
♿
Free

Notting Hill Carnival

Notting Hill, W11
Every August Bank Holiday since 1965 Notting Hill has been the scene of
London's largest and most popular arts carnival. Over 100 colourful floats, bands
and dancers wind their way through the crowded streets, filling the air with music
from South America, Africa, the Caribbean and India, not forgetting the incessant
screech of the onlookers' whistles. This heady cocktail of noise and colour is
further jazzed up with sound systems sited along the route producing their own
variations of funk, reggae, hip-hop and soul music, while stalls sell exotic foods as
well as arts and crafts.

Vibrant and exciting, this carnival is one of London's summer highlights and should not be missed. The children's day is usually held on the Sunday, with the main carnival taking place on Monday. A word of warning, though the area is always extremely crowded and provides easy pickings for thieves, so hold on to your money and leave any valuables at home.

⊖ Notting Hill and Ladbroke Grove are usually closed during the carnival, so use nearby Holland Park or Westbourne Park

🚌 12, 27, 28, 52, 94

♿

Open: early afternoon to early evening for the parades

Free

SEPTEMBER

Covent Garden Festival of Street Theatre

Covent Garden Piazza, Covent Garden, WC1 (0171 240 2255)

Every September a festival of street theatre is held to celebrate the work of all types of performers, from jugglers to dancers.

⊖ Covent Garden

🚌 6, 11, 15, 24, 29

♿

Free, but donations welcome

The Great River Race

More than 150 traditional boats take part in this spectacular event along the River Thames, from Richmond to Docklands. Viking longboats, Chinese dragonboats and Hawaiian war canoes tend to be some of the more colourful participants. The race starts from below Ham House, Richmond, at 10.00 a.m. and, having passed through central London, usually finishes at Island Gardens, opposite Greenwich Pier at around 1.00 p.m.

Start: ⊖/🚆 Richmond

🚌 33, 65, 190, 337, 391

Finish: **DLR** Island Gardens

🚌 D7, D8 (Monday–Saturday, not late evenings)

♿

Free

OCTOBER

Horse of the Year Show

Wembley Arena, Stadium Way, Wembley, Middlesex (0181 900 1234: box office)

This is another special treat for dedicated young riders.

⊖ Wembley Central, Wembley Park

🚆 Wembley Central, Wembley Stadium

🚌 18, 83, 92, 182, 224

££

Trafalgar Day Service and Parade

Trafalgar Square, WC2

The anniversary of Admiral Nelson's great sea victory at the Battle of Trafalgar (21 October 1805) is commemorated annually at 11.00 a.m. by a parade and service by over 500 Sea Cadets from all over Britain. The public can spectate.

⊖ Charing Cross, Embankment

🚊 Charing Cross

🚌 9, 11, 23, 24, 29

♿

Free

NOVEMBER

London to Brighton Veteran Car Run

This takes place on the first Sunday in November. As the cars set off from Hyde Park at 7.30 a.m., you should be there by 6.30 a.m. to have a good look round. It is sensible to take a torch as it will still be dark.

⊖ Hyde Park Corner, Marble Arch

🚌 9, 10, 14, 19, 22, 52

♿

Free

Fireworks Night

Guy Fawkes was arrested by Yeomen of the Guard on 5 November 1605, as one of the conspirators in the 'Gunpowder Plot' to blow up James I and his Parliament. The anniversary of Guy Fawkes' arrest is widely commemorated around London with bonfires and massive firework displays.

For details of organized firework displays in the London area, contact the London Tourist Board's Fireworks service from mid–October on 0839 123 401. The main, well-established annual displays, which are all free, take place in the following parks and open spaces:

Battersea Park, Prince of Wales Drive, SW11

🚊 Battersea Park

🚌 137A

♿

Bishop's Park, Fulham Palace Road, SW10

⊖ Putney Bridge

🚌 74, 220

♿

Brockwell Park, Dulwich Road, SE24

⊖ Brixton, then bus

🚊 Herne Hill, Tulse Hill

🚌 3, 37, 196

♿

Primrose Hill, NW1

🚊 Primrose Hill

⊖ Chalk Farm

🚌 274

♿

The Lord Mayor's Show

(0171 606 3030: information)

The custom dates back to 1215, when King John gave the citizens of the City of

London the special privilege of electing their own Lord Mayor rather than having to accept a royal nominee. The king, however, insisted that each Lord Mayor should present himself to the monarch at Westminster for royal approval. If the king was away (which he often was), the Lord Mayor was to report to the Law Courts, which is what happens today on the second Saturday of each November.

Viewing the Lord Mayor's Procession

Important timings along the procession route are as follows:
11.00 a.m. Head of Procession leaves Guildhall by way of
11.15 a.m. Gresham Street, Princes Street, Bank junction
11.30 a.m. St Paul's Churchyard, south side (at 12.10 p.m. the Lord Mayor is
          blessed by the Dean and Chapter of St Paul's on the West Front
          main steps of the Cathedral), Ludgate Hill, Fleet Street
11.50 a.m. Royal Courts of Justice, the Strand

returning by way of:
1.15 p.m. Temple Place, Victoria Embankment
1.25 p.m. Queen Victoria Street (by Blackfriars Bridge)
1.40 p.m. Guildhall

These times are approximate and refer to the head of the procession. The Lord Mayor's coach passes about 45 minutes after the head of the procession.
⊖ Bank (for start)
🚌 8, 11, 22B, 133
♿
Free

Christmas Lights

Christmas lights are switched on daily from dusk to midnight in Bond Street, Jermyn Street, Oxford Street and Regent Street from mid-November. The best known are the Regent Street lights, which are always first switched on by a popular celebrity.
⊖ Oxford Circus, Piccadilly Circus
🚌 3, 6, 12, 15, 25
♿
Free

DECEMBER

Pantomimes

Oh yes, you will enjoy Britain's favourite Christmas family outing. Pantomimes starring everyone's favourite celebrities are performed at theatres throughout the London area over Christmas and well into the New Year.
♿ (most venues)
££

Please take me to a Christmas show

International Show Jumping

Olympia, Hammersmith Road, W14 (0171 373 8141: box office)
Many of the big names in the world of show jumping compete in this event.
⊖ /🖳 Kensington Olympia
🚌 9, 10, 27, 28, 49
♿
££

Carol Singing and Lighting of the Christmas Tree

Trafalgar Square, WC1
Carol singing takes place every evening around the tree from early December to Christmas Eve. The tree is lit daily from dusk to midnight until Twelfth Night (6 January). Carols are sung around the tree each evening until Christmas in aid of various charities.
⊖ Charing Cross, Embankment
🖳 Charing Cross
🚌 9, 11, 23, 24, 29
♿
Free (donations to charity)

Christmas Carol Concerts

Concerts take place throughout London. To attend services at larger venues, such as Westminster Abbey and the Royal Albert Hall, you will need to buy tickets in advance. Full details of carol services can be found in December's listings magazines.

Trafalgar Square Christmas Tree

Since 1947, the city of Oslo has presented a huge Norwegian spruce Christmas tree to London as an expression of goodwill and gratitude for Britain's help during the Second World War. The tree is put up in Trafalgar Square in early December and is decorated with white lights.

Christmas Lectures

Suitable for children from eight to eighteen, the series of lectures held over the Christmas period at the Royal Institution of Great Britain, 21 Albermarle Street, W1 (0171 409 2992) were started by the scientist Michael Faraday in 1826. Their aim is for an expert to explain the essence of science in a straightforward manner. In fact the lectures are much more entertaining than that 'mission statement' sounds, and are even televised too. Recent lectures have included 'Atoms for Enquiring Minds' and 'A Journey to the Centres of the Brain'. The lectures are always popular and are booked up well in advance by schools, so phone early to ensure a seat.

Less well known but just as interesting are the lectures held at the Royal Society of Arts in John Adam Street, WC2 (0171 930 5115). Lectures are on a variety of arts- and science-related subjects and typical titles have included 'Stagecoach to Supertrain' and 'The Secrets of being a Clown'. These lectures too are suitable for children aged eight to eighteen. Lectures are also held during the Easter holidays.

⊖ Piccadilly (both venues)

🚌 3, 12, 14, 19, 38

♿ (both venues)

Free

DAYS OUT IN LONDON

The diversity of places to visit and things to do in London can be a bit daunting to both children and their parents. To help you get the most from this book, here are some ideas to steer you towards a great day out.

DAYS OUT FOR FREE (ALMOST)

Bus-top tours

If you are on a budget, it is possible to see many of the major sights of London for the cost of a family day travelcard. A Travelcard bought after 9.30 a.m. that covers zone 1 will take you by bus or tube anywhere in central London.

Museums and galleries

Many of London's museums are free, including the following: the British Museum (see page 54), Bank of England Museum (see page 62), Geffrye Museum (see page 40), the Museum of Mankind (see page 65), and the National Postal Museum (see page 65). Similarly, there is no entrance fee to the following galleries: Camden Arts Centre (see page 41), the National Gallery (see page 76), the National Museum of Cartoon Art (see page 79), the National Portrait Gallery (see page 77), the Tate Gallery (see page 78) and the Wallace Collection (see page 79).

Parks

London's parks offer an enormous variety of activities, many of which are free (see pages 125–39).

London at Work

There is more to London than the bricks and mortar of its museums, galleries and famous buildings. Over six million people live and work here in all types of occupations, from city broker to hotel chef. While most of this activity takes place behind closed doors, it is possible to glimpse at how certain people make their living.

Many fire stations will open their doors and show groups around by arrangement. Apply in writing to the London Fire Brigade, Public Relations, 8 Albert Embankment, London SE1 7SD.

See also

Tours of the Houses of Parliament (page 18)

Royal Mail

Mount Pleasant Sorting Office, Mount Pleasant, EC1 (0171 239 2313)
There are tours five times a day (Monday–Friday, 10.00 a.m.–6.00 p.m.) covering the sorting office, the mechanical sorting equipment and the 'Mail Rail', the unmanned underground trains which distribute post around London. Phone in advance to book a visit (children under nine are not admitted).
⊖ Holborn
🚌 8, 55, 68, 168, 188

THEMED DAYS OUT

Drama and Film London

a.m.   Theatre Museum, Covent Garden (see page 61).
LUNCH   Snack in Covent Garden, while watching the buskers perform.
p.m.   Over to the South Bank to visit MOMI (Museum of the Moving Image) (see page 60).
or
a.m.   Shakespeare's Globe Theatre and Museum (see page 61).
LUNCH   Lunch at Planet Hollywood in Leicester Square – check out the great film memorabilia there.
p.m.   Take in matinée performance at a West End theatre or cinema.

Toytime London

a.m.   Bethnal Green Museum of Childhood (see page 74).
LUNCH   Your own teddy bear picnic in the park (Green Park or Regent's Park are conveniently central).
p.m.   Stroll down Regent Street – a toy lover's paradise – dropping into the Disney store, the Warner Brother's store and Hamley's.
or
a.m.   Harrods' toy department – all-time favourite toys, dolls and teddy bears alongside the latest trends packed into one department
LUNCH   An ice-cream sundae or other treats at Harrods.
p.m.   London Toy and Model Museum (see page 75). Make time for a ride on their toy train outside after you have been round the museum.

Fashion London

a.m.   King's Road or Kensington High Street (particularly Kensington Market) are good places to see high street style. King's Road is also one of the few London shopping streets not to be entirely dominated by chainstores, so look out for the more interesting boutiques.
LUNCH   At the Victoria & Albert Museum café (see page 58), after a look at the gallery on the history of fashion.
p.m.   Bond Street is London's prime address for all the top fashion names – Donna Karan, Gianni Versace, Ralph Lauren and Valentino are among many of the designers you will find here.

Starstruck London

a.m.   Madame Tussaud's in Baker Street (see page 59). It's probably the closest you will get to the real stars, and the wax models are incredibly convincing.

LUNCH Planet Hollywood off Leicester Square and the Hard Rock Café (see pages 150 and 149) are both crucial places to visit for rock and film fans. Both restaurants have excellent collections of memorabilia which you can admire while you eat and they are popular haunts of visiting celebrities too.

p.m.   The exhibition at Rock Circus in the Trocadero (see page 60) is a great way of learning about the history of rock music.

Dungeons and Dragons

a.m.   London Dungeon (see page 64).

LUNCH Café in Hay's Galleria opposite the London Dungeon.

p.m.   Join a guided tour to London's ghosts. These are organized by Discovery Walks (0171 256 8973, see page 119) and are specially designed with children in mind.

or

a.m.   The Tower of London (see page 14).

LUNCH There are plenty of cafés and sandwich shops around the Tower.

p.m.   Madame Tussaud's (see page 59) – head for the Chamber of Horrors before exploring the rest of the exhibition.

or

The Natural History Museum (see page 55) – there is a whole gallery devoted to creepy-crawlies, with enough varieties to send shivers up the spine of even the most passionate insect-lover.

Planes, Trains and Cars

A day at Heathrow can be good fun, and the visitor centres are full of useful information about the planes you will see. Make sure you choose a clear day or you might be disappointed when the clouds obscure your viewing.

or

a.m.   See the Eurostar train at Waterloo station.

or

a.m.   Window shop for the car of your dreams. Among the best showrooms in London to see the ultimate fantasy cars for the playboy millionaire or millionairess are Jack Barclay in Berkeley Square for Rolls Royces and Bentleys and the McLaren showroom in Park Lane where you can see the McLaren racing car – yours for a cool £1.5 million.

LUNCH Snack in Covent Garden.

p.m.   London Transport Museum (see page 66) to see its extensive collection of all types of public transport, including trains, buses and trams.

or

p.m.   The Science Museum (see page 56), which has some excellent displays and exhibitions covering the development of the motor car.

See also London to Brighton veteran car run (page 165).

Soldiers and Sailors

(See also pages 69–71 for more ideas)

SAILORS

Greenwich is the maritime centre of London and can be approached by river boat, DLR (then underground foot tunnel) or train.

a.m.   *Cutty Sark* at Greenwich (see page 69) *or* HMS *Belfast* at London Bridge (see page 70), then a boat to Greenwich.

LUNCH   Greenwich is full of great cafés.

p.m.   National Maritime Museum and Royal Observatory (see page 71).

SOLDIERS

a.m.   The Changing of the Guard (see page 158).

LUNCH   Eating places around Buckingham Palace are pretty non-existent, so if the weather is fine, take a picnic to St James's Park or, if not, stroll up to Trafalgar Square and on to Leicester Square.

p.m.   Imperial War Museum (see page 70).

The Potted Picture Trail

Sunday afternoons are a great time to go to galleries. All London's major galleries are featured on pages 76–9 but for a quick dip into London's artistic heritage, these are the best for afternoon outings:

National Gallery – a good starting point is the information desk. Ask if they have any picture trails or quizzes available for children to follow or simply pick up a map of the gallery and borrow an audio guide (suitable for children over eight).

Tate Gallery – find the Art Trolley (see page 38) and your children can become artists for the afternoon, working on projects organized by the Tate.

Summer Days Out

Instead of competing with tourists to get into London's museums, slip off with your children for a day's outing away from the city centre. Boat cruises are relaxing and mean you don't have to worry about parking once you get to your destination. On the Thames, go downstream to Greenwich (see above) or upstream to Richmond or Hampton Court (see also page 12) from Westminster Pier. Canal cruises are great too; a particularly popular trip goes from Little Venice, stopping at London Zoo and Camden Lock (see page 117).

Other activities to enjoy in the summer include day adventure camps, playing in the park, trying out a new sport or watching free children's theatre in London's larger parks. All these activities are described in detail elsewhere in the book.

Winter Days Out

Warm museums and galleries are always more tempting when it's cold or wet outside (see Chapters One and Two). Many organize special activities for children at week-ends, half-terms and holidays too (see pages 37–48). Indoor entertainment centres, particularly the Pepsi Trocadero (see page 35), offer plenty of thrills for older children, while younger children will enjoy indoor adventure playgrounds (see page 32).

For the energetic, don't forget your local swimming pool or sports centre; ice-skating is a definite winter winner as well.

❖

SHOPPING AND SERVICES

CHAPTER TEN

SHOPPING

Whatever you want, however unusual, for your children, you are pretty likely to find it in London. From traditional prams to trendy clothes and computer games, there is an enormous wealth of specialized shops aimed at children and in the following pages, I have selected the most useful. Department stores and the larger branches of Marks & Spencer and other chains also stock a wide range of children's clothes.

You will not find any mention of schools or agencies for nannies and other domestic help. There are far too many to include and it is better to do your own research into these fields – use your friends or local authorities as a starting point.

BABY AND NURSERY GEAR

Dragons of Walton Street

23 Walton Street, Knightsbridge, SW3 (0171 589 3796)
This is a wonderful shop if you want to find something individual for your child – Rosie Fisher, the shop's proprietor, designed Prince William's nursery. Painted furniture, complete with your child's name, can either be bought from the shop or built to commission. There are also toys, clothes, bedding and other nursery equipment.
Θ South Kensington
🚌 CI, 14, 49, 74, 345
♿

Open: Monday–Friday, 9.30 a.m.–5.30 p.m.; Saturday, 10.00 a.m.–5.00 p.m.

Early Learning Centre

Kensington High Street, W8 (0171 937 0419)
A wide range of equipment, clothes, toys and accessories can be found in this branch of the Early Learning Centre – smaller branches throughout London (see telephone directory) just sell toys. You can also order direct over the phone on 01793 444844 and items will be delivered to your door.
Θ High Street Kensington
🚌 9, 10, 27, 28, 49
♿

Open: Monday–Saturday, 9.00 a.m.–6.00 p.m.; Sunday, 11.00 a.m.–5.00 p.m.

❖

Mothercare

174–176 Oxford Street, W1 (0171 636 0192)

Good-value, no-nonsense nursery equipment, plus other essentials such as clothes and toys for the newborn up to three-year-olds. Branches throughout London (see telephone directory).

⊖ Marble Arch

🚌 6, 7, 10, 15, 23

♿

Open: Monday–Friday, 9.30 a.m.–6.00 p.m. (Saturday, from 9.00 a.m.); Sunday, 12 noon–4.00 p.m.

Nursery Window

83 Walton Street, Knightsbridge, SW3 (0171 581 3358)

A limited but attractive selection of fabrics, bedding and wallpapers for the nursery, as well as a range of co-ordinated accessories.

⊖ South Kensington

🚌 C1, 14, 49, 74, 345

♿

Open: Monday–Saturday, 10.00 a.m.–5.30 p.m.

CHILDREN'S CLOTHES AND SHOES

Bananas

128 Northcote Road, Clapham, SW11 (0171 228 2384)

Children's clothes for newborns to eight-year-olds are available here, as well as a range of gifts.

🚆 Clapham Junction

🚌 91, 319 (Monday–Saturday)

♿

Open: Monday–Saturday, 9.30 a.m.–5.30 p.m.

Barney's

6 Church Road, Wimbledon, SW19 (0181 944 2915)

Clothes for newborns to ten-year-olds are comple-mented by a selection of accessories such as socks, tights and baby hats. The shop also stocks gift ideas, cards and books.

⊖ Wimbledon Park

⊖/🚆 Wimbledon

🚌 93

♿

Open: Monday–Saturday, 10.00 a.m.–6.00 p.m.; Sunday, 12 noon–5.00 p.m.

❖

Buckle My Shoe

19 St Christopher's Place, W1 (0171 935 5589)

A wide range of shoes for children, plus some styles which are also available in adult sizes.

⊖ Bond Street

🚌 6, 7, 10, 15, 23

♿

Open: Monday–Saturday, 10.00 a.m.–6.00 p.m. (Thursday, to 7.00 p.m.)

Early Clothing Centre

79–85 Fortis Green Road, Muswell Hill, N10 (0181 444 9309)

In fact two shops, Frocks Away, which sells stylish ladies' clothes, and Foot in the Door, selling children's shoes, the Early Clothing Centre was Independent Retailer of the Year 1993–4.

The shop offers a wide range of items for both categories and there is a toy box and video to keep the children amused while adults browse.

⊖ East Finchley, Highgate

🚌 102

♿

Open: Monday–Saturday, 9.30 a.m.–5.30 p.m.

Oshkosh B'Gosh

17–19 King's Road, SW3 (0171 730 1341)

Oshkosh's 'basic' selection (which includes jeans, dungarees and denim jackets) is available for children from birth to twelve years old, while its patterned collection (cotton printed dresses etc) is just for newborns to six-year-olds.

⊖ Sloane Square

🚌 C, 11, 19, 22, 211

♿

Open: Monday, Tuesday and Thursday–Saturday, 9.30 a.m.–6.00 p.m.; Wednesday, 10.00 a.m.–7.00 p.m.

Patrizia Wigan Designs

19 Walton Street, Knightsbridge, SW3 (0171 823 7080)
72 New King's Road, Fulham, SW6 (0171 736 3336)

Expensive classic clothes for children from newborns to twelve-year-olds. For babies and toddlers there are sleepsuits in either pale pink or blue.

⊖ South Kensington (Walton Street branch) Parsons Green (Fulham branch)

🚌 C1, 14, 49, 74, 345 (Knightsbridge branch); 22 (Fulham branch)

No ♿

Open: Monday–Friday, 10.00 a.m.–6.00 p.m.; Saturday, 9.00 a.m.–5.30 p.m.

Please Mum

69 New Bond Street, W1 (0171 493 5880)

Upmarket clothes at upmarket prices are available here for children from newborns to fifteen-year-olds. Most of the clothes are designer items, so it's a good place to look for special occasion clothes.

⊖ Bond Street
🚌 6, 7, 8, 15, 23
♿

Open: Monday–Saturday, 9.45 a.m.–7.00 p.m. (Thursday, to 8.00 p.m.)

Simple Smartees of Marble Arch

64 Edgware Road, W2 (0171 723 6519)
Children's clothes are available for up to eleven-year-olds. There is also a selection of nursery equipment.
⊖ Marble Arch
🚌 6, 7, 15, 16, 16A, 23
♿

Open: Monday–Saturday, 10.00 a.m.–7.00 p.m.

Smartees

5 Bellevue Parade, Wiseton Road, Wandsworth Common, SW17 (0181 672 3392)
Particularly noted for its selection of boys' clothes, Smartees also sells books, toys, gift ideas, party invitations and giftwrap.
🚆 Wandsworth Common
🚌 91, 219
♿

Open: Monday–Saturday, 9.30 a.m.–5.30 p.m.

Teddy B's

62 Barnes High Street, SW13 (0181 878 7338)
The sister shop to Barney's in Wimbledon (see page 175), Teddy B's stocks children's clothes for newborns to eight-year-olds as well as a selection of gifts and accessories.
⊖ Hammersmith, then bus
🚆 Barnes Bridge
🚌 9A (Monday–Saturday, not evenings), R69 (Monday–Saturday, shopping hours)
♿

Open: Monday–Saturday, 10.00 a.m.–5.30 p.m.

Young England

47 Elizabeth Street, Pimlico, SW1 (0171 259 9003)
Traditional children's clothes and nursery goods made in Great Britain, with the emphasis on traditional.
⊖ Sloane Square, Victoria
🚌 C1, 11
♿

Open: Monday–Friday, 9.30 a.m.–5.30 p.m.

❖

NEARLY NEW CLOTHES

Little Gems
59 Vernon Road, East Sheen, SW14 (0181 742 3152)
An agency for new and nearly new designer and good-quality clothes for newborns to sixteen-year-olds, equipment and toys. Haircuts by appointment.
🚇 Mortlake
🚌 33, R69 (Monday–Saturday, shopping hours), 337
♿

Open: Monday–Saturday, 9.00 a.m.–5.00 p.m.
(Saturday, to 4.30 p.m.)

Scarecrow
131 Walham Green Court, Moore Park Road, Fulham, SW6 (0171 381 1023)
Two floors of finest-quality second-hand clothes, toys, books and nursery equipment. A large selection of formal, sports and fun clothing for newborns to fifteen-year-olds.
⊖ Fulham Broadway
🚌 11, 14, 28, 211, 295
♿

Open: Monday–Friday, 10.00 a.m.–5.00 p.m.; Saturday, 9.30 a.m.–1.00 p.m.

Swallows and Amazons
91 Nightingale Lane, Wandsworth, SW12 (0181 673 0275)
A large selection of nearly new clothes and baby equipment. Children's hairdressing is available on most afternoons and some Saturdays.
🚇 Wandsworth Common
🚌 91
♿

Open: Monday–Saturday, 9.30 a.m.–5.30 p.m.

TOYS, GAMES AND GIFTS

Cheeky Monkeys
202 Kensington Park Road, W11 (0171 292 9021)
Attractive handmade toys, educational toys, second-hand clothes and clothes for dressing up are available here.
⊖ Notting Hill
🚌 52, 302
♿

Open: Monday–Friday, 9.30 a.m.–5.30 p.m. (Saturday, from 10.00 a.m.)

Childsplay

112 Tooting High Street, SW17 (0181 672 6470)
The toys you will find here have been selected by people who work with children and have hands-on experience of what children actually enjoy playing with. As a result you won't see cheap, gimmicky toys, but dolls, teasets and craft materials (such as glue, sequins and coloured paper), as well as games, books and puzzles.

θ Tooting Broadway

🚌 57, 155

♿

Open: daily, 10.00 a.m.–5.00 p.m. (Wednesday, to 2.00 p.m.)

Hamley's

188–196 Regent Street, W1 (0171 734 3161)
3 The Market Piazza, Covent Garden, WC2 (0171 240 4646)
Hamley's in Regent Street is one of the world's largest toy shops and has an excellent range of toys from the traditional to the latest products.

θ Oxford Circus (Regent Street), Covent Garden

🚌 12, 15, 38, 88, 139

No ♿ (Covent Garden)

♿ (Regent Street)

Open: Monday–Saturday, 9.30 a.m.–7.00 p.m. (Thursday–Saturday, to 8.00 p.m.);
Sunday, 12 noon–6.00 p.m.

The Hill Toy Company

71 Abingdon Road, W8 (0171 937 8797)
Beautifully crafted toys that are built to last include wooden castles, puppet theatres, wooden farms and trains sets. Smaller items include skipping ropes, craft kits and traditional games, such as bagatelle. Toys are available by mail order too on 01765 689955.

θ High Street Kensington

🚌 9, 10, 27, 28, 49

♿

Open: Monday–Saturday, 9.00 a.m.–5.30 p.m.

The London Dolls' House Company

29 The Market, Covent Garden, WC2 (0171 240 8681)
Dolls' houses for adults and children are available. Most of the dolls' house furniture and contents would be too fragile for children to play with, but there is a small selection which is suitable.

θ Covent Garden

🚌 1, 9, 68, 176, 501

♿

Open: Monday–Saturday, 10.00 a.m.–7.00 p.m.; Sunday, 12 noon–5.00 p.m.

Patrick's Toys

107–111 Lillie Road, SW6 (0171 385 9864)
Here you will find the latest toy crazes, as well as models and craft materials.

⊖ Fulham Broadway, then bus
🚌 74, 190, 211, 295
♿

Open: Monday–Saturday, 9.15
a.m.–5.45 p.m.

The Play Shop

327 Upper Street, Islington, N1
(0171 704 0756)
Unusual wooden toys, soft toys
and children's clothes are available here.
There is also a children's hairdresser.
⊖ Angel
🚌 4, 19, 30, 43
♿

Open: Monday–Saturday, 9.30 a.m.–5.30 p.m. (Saturday, to 6.00 p.m.)

Smartees

See page 177

Tridias

25 Bute Street, South Kensington, SW7 (0171 584 2330)
6 Lichfield Terrace, Sheen Road, Richmond (0181 948 3459)
This shop succeeds in achieving the almost impossible, by offering toys that
parents like the look of and children enjoy playing with. Most of the toys are
wooden, but this does not mean they are boring, as here you will find a wealth of
toys and puzzles, some in plain wood and others coloured. There is also a range
of jewellery and bead kits and a Design-A-Hairband for the fashion-conscious
little girl. If you prefer, you can order by telephone (01225 469455) from their
excellent mail order catalogue.
⊖ South Kensington (Bute Street branch); Richmond (Richmond branch)
🚆 Richmond (Richmond branch)
🚌 C1, 49 (Bute Street branch); 33, 337 (Richmond branch)
♿

Open: Monday–Friday, 9.30 a.m.–6.00 p.m. (Saturday, from 10.00 a.m.)

Trotters

34 King's Road, SW3 (0171 259 9620)
Clothes for newborns to ten-year-olds and toys are available. There is also a
children's hairdresser.
⊖ Sloane Square
🚌 C1, 11, 22, 49, 211
♿

Open: Monday–Saturday, 9.00 a.m.–6.30 p.m. (Wednesday, to 7.00 p.m.)

THEME STORES

The Disney Store

140 Regent Street, W1 (0171 287 6558)

The first such theme store to hit London, this shop has hundreds of toys and other merchandise relating to Disney's favourite characters.

⊖ Piccadilly Circus

🚌 3, 6, 15, 23, 88

♿

Open: Monday–Saturday, 9.30 a.m.–8.00 p.m.; Sunday, 12 noon–6.00 p.m.

Warner Brothers Studio Store

178–192 Regent Street, W1 (0171 434 3334)

Bugs Bunny and other Warner cartoon characters are the stars of this shop.

⊖ Piccadilly Circus

🚌 3, 12, 14, 19, 38

♿

Open: Monday–Saturday, 10.00 a.m.–7.00 p.m. (Thursday and Saturday, to 8.00 p.m.); Sunday, 12 noon–6.00 p.m.

BOOKS

Books for Children

97 Wandsworth Bridge Road, SW6 (0171 384 1821)

A selection of books suitable from birth to early teenage are packed into the two floors of this shop.

⊖ Fulham Broadway, then bus

🚌 28, 295

♿ (ground floor only)

Open: Monday–Friday, 9.30 a.m.–6.00 p.m. (Monday, from 10.00 a.m.); Saturday, 9.30 a.m.–5.30 p.m.

Children's Book Centre

237 Kensington High Street, W8 (0171 937 7497)

The range of books spans the years from babyhood to teenage. Videos and CD-ROM are also available. Special events such as author readings are held regularly in this long-established shop.

⊖ High Street Kensington

🚌 9, 10, 27, 28, 49

♿

Open: Monday, Wednesday, Friday and Saturday, 9.30 a.m.–6.30 p.m.; Tuesday, 9.30 a.m.–6.00 p.m.; Thursday, 9.30 a.m.–7.00 p.m.; Sunday, 12 noon–6.00 p.m.

GO HOME WITH A BOOK

Children's Bookshop

29 Fortis Green Road, Muswell Hill, N10 (0181 444 5500)
Fabric books to teenage novels are all available here, as well as a selection of audio cassettes.

⊖ East Finchley, Highgate, then bus
🚌 102, 143
&

Open: Monday–Friday, 9.15 a.m.–5.45 p.m. (Saturday, to 5.30 p.m.); Sunday, 12 noon–5.00 p.m.

Comic Showcase

76 Neal Street, WC2 (0171 240 3664)
Heaven for the cartoon enthusiast, this shop specializes in American comics. There are also cartoon books, science fiction and associated goodies, such as T-shirts and toys.

⊖ Covent Garden
🚌 6, 11, 15, 24, 29
&

Open: daily, 10.00 a.m.–7.00 p.m. (Monday–Wednesday, to 6.00 p.m.)

Forbidden Planet

71 New Oxford Street, WC1 (0171 836 4179)
Forbidden Planet is to science fiction, fantasy and horror what the Comic Showcase (see above) is to comics. Both adult and children's books are available here.

⊖ Tottenham Court Road
🚌 8, 24, 25, 29, 55
&

Open: Monday–Saturday, 10.00 a.m.– 6.00 p.m. (Thursday and Friday, to 7.00 p.m.)

Marchpane

16 Cecil Court, WC2 (0171 836 8661)
Not strictly a shop for children, but both adults and children will love the stunning collection of illustrated children's books offered here.

⊖ Leicester Square
🚌 24, 29, 176
&

Open: Monday–Saturday, 10.30 a.m.–
6.30 p.m.

CRAFTS

Markets

Covent Garden market and Camden Town market are excellent hunting grounds for handmade jewellery and gifts and clothes. In the summer both these areas attract hair-plaiters – you can get yours plaited with colourful ribbons for just a few pounds!

Bead Shop

43 Neal Street, WC2 (0171 240 0931)

Make your own necklace and other jewellery by buying a selection of colourful beads. Accessories are available too.

θ Covent Garden

🚌 6, 11, 15, 24, 29

&

Open: Monday, 1.00 p.m.–6.00 p.m.; Tuesday – Friday, 10.30 a.m.–6.00 p.m.; Saturday, 11.30 a.m.–5.00 p.m.

Potterycraft

8–10 Ingate Place, SW8 (0171 720 0050)

All the equipment a potter needs (young or old), from clays and glazes to tools and kilns.

θ Sloane Square, then bus

🚉 Queenstown Road

🚌 137 (Monday–Saturday, not evenings), 137A (Monday–Friday, peak hours and Sunday)

&

Open: Monday–Saturday, 9.00 a.m.–5.00 p.m.

Winsor & Newton

51 Rathbone Place, W1 (0171 636 4231)

Art equipment for the professional and amateur, with plenty of affordable paints and tools for the young artist.

θ Oxford Circus, Tottenham Court Road

🚌 6, 7, 10, 15, 23

&

Open: Monday–Saturday, 9.00 a.m.–5.30 p.m. (Saturday, to 5.00 p.m.)

SERVICES

A wide variety of entertainers and venues is available in London for children's parties, geared to all ages and tastes. A couple of shops are also included where you can find a miscellany of party equipment.

PARTY ENTERTAINERS

Animal Krackers
32 Chase Road, Epsom, Surrey (01372 742880)
These party entertainers will turn up at your party as a variety of animal characters, such as the White Rabbit, a tiger, a bear, the Pink Panther and Father Christmas. They are bookable for a minimum of 2 hours.

Carolyn James
12 York Road, Richmond, Surrey (0181 940 8407)
This party entertainer offers a selection of themes for a party, from puppets to face-painting. Also available are parties with themes, such as Aladdin, Camelot and Cinderella.

The Clown Collective
52 Herga Road, Wealdstone (0181 861 0919)
This agency can provide a selection of entertainers who offer a range of clown activities, as well as face-painting. They can also arrange workshops in circus skills and fire shows.

Comedygrams
180 Ellerton Road, Surbiton, Surrey (0181 399 6007)
This agency specializes in visits from a cartoon character, but will also organize face-painters or even a circus workshop.

Crêchendo
St Luke's Hall, Adrian Mews, Ifield Road, SW10 (0171 259 2727)
As well as running pre-school gyms, Crêchendo organize entertainments for all ages from first birthday parties to active gym parties and glamorous disco parties for older children. They can do the catering too and also hire out bouncy castles.

Diane's Puppets

9 Mercury Court, Southey Road, SW9 (0181 820 946)

Diane's Puppets perform interactive puppet shows, as well as offering face-painting, songs and stories.

Fizzie Lizzie

41 Eastlake House, Frampton Street, NW8 (0171 723 3877)

Fizzie Lizzie is a female clown whose act includes puppetry, bubbles, games, plate spinning, juggling and other circus skills (for children and adults). She also runs the country's only clown gallery, which has an exhibition of clown memorabilia.

Merlin Entertainments

29 Norwood Drive, North Harrow (0181 866 6327)

This firm will help you choose the entertainer that's just right for your child's party. The full package includes games, dancing, competitions, prizes and a Magic and Fun show.

Tiddlywinks

28 Fulham Park Gardens, SW6 (0171 726 1842)

Tiddlywinks are two actresses who can turn a children's party into a theatrical event. They organize interactive children's parties aimed at three- to seven-year-olds and enlist their help to stage a play.

Twizzle Entertainment

31 Lillian Road, Barnes, SW13 (0181 748 3138)

This is an agency that can supply all a party's needs, from a Batmobile to pony rides, as well as a bouncy castle and magicians.

PARTY EQUIPMENT

The Farmyard

54 Friars Stile Road, Richmond (0181 332 0038)

This is a party shop which can supply party bags on any theme and for a range of budgets.

θ/🚉 Richmond

🚌 337, 391

Open: Monday–Saturday, 9.30 a.m.–5.30 p.m.

The Party Shop

268 Lavender Hill, Clapham, SW11 (0171 924 3210)

As well as offering party items, this shop hires out fancy dress.

🚉 Clapham Junction

🚌 35, 39, 156, 170, 295

Open: Monday–Saturday, 9.00 a.m.–6.00 p.m. (Thursday, to 7.00 p.m.)

PARTY VENUES

Chelsea Football Club
Stamford Bridge, Fulham Road, SW10 (0171 385 0710)
Fulham Football Club
Craven Cottage, Stevenage Road, SW6 (0171 736 6561)
Both clubs will arrange birthday parties to include football coaching,
a signed football, a tour of the ground and a surprise guest.

⊖ Fulham Broadway
(Chelsea); Putney Bridge
(Fulham)

🚌 11, 211 (Chelsea);
C4, 74, 220 (Fulham)

♿

Discovery Zone
The Junction Shopping Centre, Clapham Junction, SW11 (0171 223 1717)
See also page 33
Birthday parties can be held here. Special party bags and ice-cream for each child
will be provided (for a fee).

🚊 Clapham Junction

🚌 35, 39, 156, 170, 295

Limited ♿ (phone in advance)

Jubilee Sports Centre
Caird Street, W10 (0181 960 9629)
See also page 97
'Splash' parties in your own section of the swimming pool, filled with rafts and
pool toys. Team games in the sports hall afterwards. Also offered is a 'Fit Kids'
party in the gym, with inflatable raft and Captain Hoppy.

⊖ Queens Park

🚌 18, 36

♿

London Zoo
Regent's Park, NW1 (0171 586 3339)
See also page 106
A birthday tea in a private room, a tour of the
zoo with special animal encounters, face-
painting and animals masks available too.

⊖ Regent's Park

🚌 13, 18, 27, 82, 113

♿

McDonald's
See page 155

Pippa Pop-ins

430 Fulham Road, SW6 (0171 385 2457)

In a bright yellow Georgian house on the border of Chelsea and Fulham, Pippa Pop-ins is a wonderful combination of kindergarten, nursery school and even a hotel for two- to twelve-year-olds. Parties can also be held here, from traditional tea parties to an adventure party with barbecues and an assault course.

Pippa Pop-ins also offers exciting holiday excursions and a children's school run to various schools with afternoon tea.

⊖ Fulham Broadway

🚌 11, 14, 211

♿

Playscape Pro-Racing

See page 86

Polka Theatre for Children

240 The Broadway, Wimbledon, SW19 (0181 543 3741)

See also page 144

A trip to the theatre, then a party with a cake.

⊖/🚆 Wimbledon

🚌 57, 93, 155

♿

Raffles Townhouse

287 King's Road, Chelsea, SW3 (0171 352 1091)

Disco parties in the 'nightclub', or theme parties with tea and a magician.

⊖ Sloane Square

🚌 C1, 11, 22, 49, 211

♿

UCI Cinema

Whiteleys of Bayswater, Queensway, W2 (0171 792 3303)

A film, a meal, a party hat, sunglasses and an 'It's my Birthday' badge, for little more than the cost of a cinema ticket. The popcorn was voted the best in London, according to a survey carried out by *Time Out* magazine.

⊖ Bayswater, Queensway

🚌 12, 23, 36, 70, 94

♿

Unicorn Arts Theatre

6 Great Newport Street, WC2 (0171 379 3280)

See also pages 38 and 145

Extremely popular birthday workshops with a theme of your choice are held in a rehearsal room. A specialized leader is provided by the theatre.

⊖ Leicester Square

🚌 24, 29, 176

No ♿

COUNSELLING AND ADVICE

Action for Sick Children
Argyle House, 29–31 Euston Road, NW1 (0171 833 2041)
Advice and information for parents and carers of sick children.

Childline
Freepost 111, Islington, N1 (0800 1111)
A helpline for children who need support and advice.

Gingerbread
35 Wellington Street, WC2 (0171 240 0953)
Association for single-parent families and information about local groups.

Kidsline
0171 222 8070
Information on children's classes, clubs, events, sports and entertainment
in London.
Open: term-time, weekdays, 4.00 p.m.–6.00 p.m.; school holidays, weekdays,
9.00 a.m.–4.00 p.m.

Parents Anonymous
Manor Gardens Centre, 6–9 Manor Gardens, Islington, N7 (0171 263 8918)
Helpline for parents in need of emotional support.

Parents at Work
77 Holloway Road, Islington, N7 (0171 500 5771)
Practical advice and support groups on childcare and related issues.

INDEX

PICTURE CREDITS